THE meditation doctor

THE meditation doctor

Martina
Glasscock
Barnes

COLLINS & BROWN

First published in Great Britain in 2004
by Collins & Brown Limited
The Chrysalis Building
Bramley Road
London W10 6SP

An imprint of **Chrysalis** Books Group plc

1 3 5 7 9 8 6 4 2

British Library Cataloguing-in-Publication Data:
A catalogue record for this book is available from the British Library.

ISBN 1-84340-088-X

Copy-edited by Michele Turney
Designed by Gemma Wilson
Illustrations by Kang and Trina D.
Photography by Sian Irvine
Proofread by Mandy Greenfield

Reproduction by Classicscan, Singapore
Printed and bound by Imago, Singapore

Contents

Foreword

Nearly 40 years ago Maharishi Mahesh Yogi taught the Beatles to meditate and the popularization of meditation in the Western world began. The practice of meditation elsewhere is ancient. It can be positively dated back to 2000 to 3000 B.C. in the Hindu tradition. Some experts believe that its roots are actually pre-historic, practiced by the shamans of hunter-gatherer tribes many thousands of years ago.

While continuing to grow in popularity as a part of many traditional and non-traditional spiritual practices, awareness of the usefulness of meditative techniques in the area of physical and psychological health is also rapidly growing. This awareness is supported by the direct clinical experience of thousands of individual health practitioners as well as an ever-growing body of scientific literature. It is increasingly clear that the effects of the mind on the body and of the body on the mind are so profound that to consider them to be separate entities is no longer practical from the medical viewpoint. Most people recognize that what we put into our bodies and how we treat them in other ways has a powerful effect on how we think and feel. It is equally true that what is happening in our mind scan have a major impact on our physical health.

The use of relaxation, meditation, guided imagery, and related techniques is wonderfully available. One need not subscribe to a new philosophy or religion, retreat to a monastery, or convert to an Eastern practice of meditation. You don't have to be a certain age, be wealthy, creative, strong, or anything else in particular to benefit from

meditation. The techniques are easily accessible and can be done wherever you can find a quiet environment—at work, home, or on holiday—to practice in. When practiced regularly, even a single, consciously focused breath can be remarkably calming. Stopping for traffic lights or even standing in line at the grocery store can be opportunities for such a mini-relaxation.

I have been in the practice of general psychiatry for over 20 years. People come to me for the "medical" (which usually translates as medication) part of their treatment. Whatever brings them to me— unresolved grief, severe chronic illnesses or obsessive-compulsive disorder—the question of how to manage stress better almost always arises. "Don't sweat the small stuff, and remember, it's all small stuff," is great advice, but how do you actually do that? When the kids are running riot, or somebody cuts you off in traffic nearly killing you, or you're worried that money is tight, how can you find a place of calmness? Many stressors are unavoidable. Very often our first reaction to them is a building anger, even to the point of rage. In this frame of mind we often react poorly, without thinking clearly, and put ourselves in an even more stressful situation. This will of course magnify the "mind" symptoms of the conditions I treat, not to mention "body" symptoms such as increasing blood pressure, gastric acidity and muscle tension, to name but a few.

To answer this need in my practice, I frequently teach a meditative relaxation technique. Having practiced meditation myself in one form or another for about 35 years, I have a deep confidence in its capacity to effect powerful, lasting change in how we respond to stressful events, as well as its positive effect on our "background stress level," or attitudes. I try to instruct my patients that it is our response to stress, not the stress itself, that can harm us or help us grow.

I can think of many success stories of the benefits of regular meditation in my patients. One stands out in particular because of my own lack of confidence in my patient's capacity for healing in this way. I first met this patient on a locked psychiatric unit where she had been involuntarily hospitalized, secondary to a psychotic episode that included an outburst of rage with near-tragic consequences to her family. Because of her previous history, it seemed unlikely to me that she would be able to continue successfully in her family and community without the indefinite use of anti-depressant and anti-psychotic medications. Her focus, however, during her hospital stay was on diet (a healthy vegetarian one, nothing unusual) and meditation. Once out of hospital she soon requested that her medication was reduced, and I was left with the choice of following her and reducing her medications too rapidly (I thought) or having her do it on her own. I chose to follow her, figuring that at least I would be in a better position to help when she relapsed. She never did. Five years later, taking only a tiny dose of medication, she continues to do well. I do not suggest that meditation is a reasonable stand-alone treatment for psychosis, but in her particular case the improvement was quite dramatic.

In many ways, the more mundane examples I see daily, in which conflicts are dealt with more healthily, or negative thoughts challenged successfully, are more important. They happen all the time, with little fanfare, and are immensely healing. My own observations support what the scientific literature is increasingly demonstrating: people who utilize these techniques regularly do better. Their improvement sustains, and they often have less need for medication.

Martina Glasscock Barnes, with *The Meditation Doctor*, makes an important and timely contribution to mainstream public access to mind/body techniques. Long a practitioner and inspiring teacher of meditative methods herself, Martina takes a vast and complex subject and grounds it through techniques that are practical and to the point. The book is beautifully written and easy to understand. Drawing on a multitude of sources and traditions, *The Meditation Doctor* will appeal to people with a wide variety of backgrounds and needs. If you are new to meditation and relaxation, this book is a good place to start. Experienced meditators will benefit from the specific, condition-focused techniques that Martina communicates so clearly. Martina has done an excellent job of capturing the essential elements of meditation and directing them into specific techniques to address particular ailments that are known to respond well to meditation.

In the scientific literature, people with depression show a significant decrease in relapse rate when meditation is added to their treatment plan. The techniques used here to treat depression effectively target key components that can contribute to depression. Anxiety, a common response to stress, has been shown to respond as effectively to the regular daily practice of meditation as it does to medication, with no pharmacy bills and no medication side effects. The regular use of any of the relaxation techniques in *The Meditation Doctor*, as well as the specific one for treating anxiety, promise to be highly effective in helping to reduce and manage anxiety.

Headaches have also responded well to meditation and relaxation techniques as given in the book. (One more anecdotal report: a family physician friend and colleague of mine, not tolerating or responding to mainstream treatment for her migraine headaches, is now improving using a technique very similar to the one Martina describes later in these pages.) This is also true for the treatment of chronic pain: medications can often be reduced or even discontinued with the use of a relaxation program. When used regularly, the techniques given for chronic pain offer hope and potential to bring pain relief. Meditation improves the immune response, as demonstrated by increased antibody production after flu shots, as well as in studies showing increased tumor-fighting cells in cancer patients. Time spent working consciously with enhancing the immune response is time well spent. The usefulness of meditation in treating hypertension (high blood pressure) is well documented. The list of potential benefits goes on and on, including use in seemingly unconnected conditions such as ulcer disease, chronic heart disease, attention deficit disorder, irritable bowel syndrome, migraine and tension headaches, antisocial behavior, and asthma.

More difficult to define and measure is the profound sense of peacefulness, awareness, and wellbeing that many practitioners of meditative techniques report. This experience often begins during meditation sessions, and expands increasingly as practice is continued. It is difficult to describe and for me is the essence of the meditative experience.

Quiet your mind, open your heart, and enjoy your Self.

Ken Lexington MD

Introduction

Meditation in some form or another is an ancient practice found across cultures and religions. Most ancient cultures developed songs, chants, and rituals to manipulate consciousness to connect with a higher power. Often this was in the form of sound. For example, Native Americans use ceremonial chants like the Hindu mantra (repeated words to achieve an altered state of mind) as a form of prayerful meditation.

There is a rich library of Gregorian chants. Roman Catholics have sacred music, use incantations, and make use of repetitive words when reciting Hail Mary on rosary beads. Christians use prayer, devotional songs, and meditation on the scriptures. The Hebrew Kabbalah makes use of incantation. These oral customs offer a rich history of teachings. The teachings have been passed down into different forms of meditation.

The techniques in *The Meditation Doctor* draw on diverse cultural traditions including Tibetan and Zen Buddhism, Native American ritual, Kundalini, Tantric, and Hatha yoga, Hindu-based meditations, esoteric Christianity, Jewish Kabbalah, Taoist Chi Gong, and Polynesian Huna.

Basic Techniques

Mind/Body Connection

Eastern medicine and philosophy have known for centuries what Western medicine has only recently begun to understand and accept with scientific certainty: the mind and body cannot be separated. The status of the mind affects the body, and the status of the body influences the mind. They are in a continual state of communication.

The mind's influence is such that psychology can become physiology. For example, when an individual perceives danger, fearful thoughts are translated into biochemical responses. The brain releases stress hormones, triggering the defensive "fight or flight" response. A loved one's death can trigger this same biochemical response, sending the mind/body into a high state of alert. A similar reaction can occur when people lose their jobs.

If this state of heightened alert continues, it can develop into chronic mental or emotional stress. This in turn can lead to anxiety, depression, fatigue, or a host of other physical symptoms. The converse, however, is also true. Positive thoughts produce healing body reactions. Maintaining a positive outlook, thinking of someone you love, or engaging in an activity you enjoy stimulates the brain to produce endorphins, the body's natural painkillers.

As we understand the role the mind can play in healing, people are seeking avenues to strengthen the mind/body connection as a means of taking charge of their health. Meditation is a powerful and natural medium that fosters communication between the mind and body to achieve health and wellness. The body is inherently intelligent and continually seeking to achieve homeostasis (balance). Through meditation, the body regains inner balance and instinctively taps into the original "blueprint" of wellness to heal itself.

I hope that you will find the meditations in this book to be intelligent, thoughtful, and logical. While these techniques may not "cure" an ailment or condition, they may move the practitioner into a greater level of healing. Healing is not synonymous with curing. Healing essentially means achieving "wholeness." Healing can be the achievement of a higher level of wholeness and restoration than previously experienced.

Good Health

The Chinese characters for good health combine the symbols for "standing person" and "movement" with "water," which nourishes and teaches us to flow. Proper nourishment, movement, and attitude bring good health.

Tips for Building a Healthy Mind/Body Connection

- Learn to listen to the inner messages your body gives you and respect when it is time to eat, slow down, rest, or play.
- Follow a nutritious diet.
- Drink plenty of water: 8–10 glasses daily.
- Identify the stressors in your life and see if some may be reduced or eliminated.
- Evaluate current commitments. Are they worth the energy invested?
- Be mindful of the expectations you place upon yourself. Create realistic expectations.
- Schedule time just for yourself to use as you please.
- Reduce external stimulation. For example, read a book rather than watch television.
- Create time to reflect on and review your daily choices.
- Pursue activities that are pleasurable and for which you have a passion.
- Allow time for contemplation, prayer, visualization, or meditation.
- Maintain an attitude of realistic optimism.

The universal life force is the vital force that sustains all life. It is the greater intelligence that permeates and flows through all matter—animate and inanimate—throughout the universe. This supreme and animating universal force is what nourishes life. It is thought to possess the qualities of harmony, balance, compassion, and unconditional love.

Universal Life Force

Universal life force has many names. In Indian philosophy, the Sanskrit name is *prana*. In Chinese culture, the essence of life is called *qi* or *chi* (pronouned chee). The mystic Judaic tradition of Kabbalah calls the force that animates the human body the astral light. In the West, the words life force, vital force, breath of life, or spirit all give reference to this universal life force. In this book I will refer to this force as chi or energy.

Chi is the permeating energetic force that gives and sustains life. It is found within all atoms, from the smallest of microscopic cells within the body to the billions of stars within the expansive universe. Everything is composed of energy. We live in an interconnected sea of chi. The universal laws, which govern energy, can be understood as a hierarchical system. This hierarchy ranges from the densest to the most subtle energy matrix. The body can be seen as a miniature reflection of the universe as it contains a dense physical matrix governed by a range of subtle energy levels.

Yoga postures and meditative techniques have a positive impact on the energy of these subtle bodies, enabling us to create positive physical, emotional, and mental changes. For example, when doing a yoga pose, the movement of body fluids through the circulatory system is enhanced. Likewise, meditation can cause biochemical changes in the body that initiate a relaxation response.

Relaxation is a vital antidote to stress. The word "relax" originates from the Latin word *relaxare,* meaning "to loosen." Relaxation promotes deep rest in which there is no movement or effort and the brain is in a quiet state. This relaxation response results in profound and positive physiological changes. Relaxation decreases the heart rate, blood pressure, respiration rate, muscle tension, metabolic rate, and oxygen consumption.

Vital Centers of the Body

In Eastern philosophy, the body is believed to contain a complex system of subtle energy centers that play an essential role in the health of the physical, emotional, mental, and spiritual self. When an individual is healthy on all these levels, these centers spin in harmony and are balanced within. The Sanskrit word for these energy centers is *chakra* (pronounced with a hard "ch" as in "chalk"), which derives its meaning from the words "moving wheel." These chakras are sometimes referred to as "wheels of light."

We have seven main chakras or energy centers present in both the ethereal (energy) body and physical body. These centers align vertically along the spine and are composed of high-frequency energy strands that are perceived as light to the mystic's eye. From the base of the spine moving upward, the chakras are the base, sacral, solar plexus, heart, throat, brow, and crown. These chakras are interpreted as wheels of light containing small rotating vortices or petals. Thus the centers are referred to as lotus flowers with the number of petals ranging from four at the root center to one thousand at the crown center. Enlightened individuals, such as Buddha or Christ, can activate the light of all one thousand petals, thereby creating a halo of light around their head.

The energy centers in our body are vital to balancing our inner world with the external environment. They draw in universal life force and function as pathways to receive energy, metabolize it, and distribute it to the major nerve plexus nearest to each chakra. This life force is translated into electrical impulses within the central nervous system and endocrine glands that distribute life force to the major organs within the body.

The health of the chakra system depends on the physical, emotional, mental, and spiritual state of the individual. There are different ways in which the chakra system can become imbalanced, damaged, or blocked. Fear, anxiety, emotional upset, dramatic loss, or major life changes can cause a disturbance in the energy flow. Stress is a key culprit. Chronic stress can occur from simply living a fast-paced and demanding life. Unfortunately, this may cause the chakra system, and subsequently the nervous system, to become chronically overstimulated. The overall effect is that the body becomes exhausted and depleted. This can lead to illness and the inability to support proper emotional and mental capacities.

Regular meditation along with rest, proper nutrition, and regular exercise help to balance these vital centers.

Sahasrara
Crown

Ajna
Brow

Vissuddha
Throat

Anahata
Heart

Manipura
Pancreas
Solar Plexus

Swadisthana
Sacral/over the
Spleen

Muladhara
Base/genital

Getting Started

What are Meditation, Imagery, and Visualization?

Meditation practices vary across diverse cultural traditions. Meditation is a mental process of moving the physical body into relaxation in order to achieve deep states of concentration that give rise to calmness, stability of attention, and insight.

Meditation can be concentrative, which Buddhists call *samadhi* practices, or insightful, which are known as *vipassana* practices. Meditation can be passive or active. In general, Western meditation tends to be active, whereas Eastern tends to be passive or receptive. Visualization / guided imagery is a form of meditation in which one evokes a heightened awareness and sensitivity through directed concentration and intent. It can include all the senses in addition to visual. The practitioner can imagine something from the mind's eye as well as from physical, auditory, or tactile sensation.

Healing meditation asks the individual to focus on specific techniques to achieve desired results such as increasing communication between the mind and body, reducing pain, enhancing the immune response. The healing meditations in this book focus on enhancing vital energy as well as moving energy blocks that contribute to illness through reference to energy centers (Hindu), energy meridians (Chinese), or states of concentration, intent and imagery (Western).

It is not necessary to adopt any particular religion or philosophy to take up meditation practice. The techniques are not meant to compete with or replace your current philosophies, but simply to enhance the connection between your mind and body. If you have a religious or spiritual philosophy, meditation can enhance and deepen your connection to your spiritual ideals and higher power.

The meditation techniques contained in this book are not intended to diagnose or cure physical, emotional, or mental illness or disorders. They are designed to be used alongside, and to enhance, conventional treatment.

- Meditating is not a substitute for proper health care.
- Please consult your physician or primary health-care provider before beginning any exercises in this book.
- If your symptoms become aggravated or worsen while using the techniques, stop and consult your physician.
- Do not meditate if you have experienced recent emotional or mental illness.

How to Use This Book

The first part of the book introduces basic meditation techniques that can be used on their own or in combination with the other therapeutic techniques. Part 2 offers techniques to treat physical ailments. Part 3 addresses psychological ailments that can result in physical symptoms.

There are two levels of difficulty indicated in the icon headings of each exercise. Under the Level heading there is a brief descriptor of difficulty level. In general, Level 1 is a beginner level that is easily executed. Level 2 is a more advanced level, affording you the opportunity to address the ailment at a deeper level.

Level 2 most often requires the ability to sustain concentration and focus. Practice and repetition build these skills. It is recommended that you familiarize yourself with the Basic Techniques in Part I as well as with Concentration and Focus and Centering and Inner Balance. This will build a strong base for all other meditations in the book.

In each icon heading you will see cross-reference. This indicates what technique should be used with the meditation, such as a recommendation for a particular breathing technique, or body or hand position. Use the index to locate these techniques. Look out for Quick Remedies if you are seeking a simple and short exercise. If you do not attain desired results with Quick Remedy, try another meditation under the same heading.

Read through the technique you wish to use several times. Then record it on tape or have someone whose voice you enjoy record it for you. Repetitive practice will enable you to activate these techniques through memory.

If you are new to visualization or meditation, the following guidelines may be helpful:
- Choose a quiet place to practice, free from any distractions.
- Turn off the ringer on the phone.
- If at any time you become uncomfortable, simply end the visualization or pose and try again later.
- Practice a technique on a regular basis. If your condition is chronic, try practicing a particular meditation for 21 days in a row.
- Keep a journal or log of your experiences.
- Be patient and gentle with yourself.

Meditation can be carried out while stationary, in a sitting posture. Or, it can be in the form of movement, such as yoga, t'ai chi, or chi gong. This book contains both sitting and moving techniques.

The techniques can also be described as concentrative or receptive in nature. A concentrative approach is one in which you focus the mind in a particular direction. A receptive approach is one in which you cultivate the qualities of mindfulness and observation. The concentrative techniques focus the mind to heal particular ailments. The receptive techniques assist the mind and inner self to become receptive to new perceptions and insights to heal the body.

A proper mental attitude is a key element of meditation. Strive to release expectations about the results of meditation and focus rather on the commitment and intention you invest in the various poses and techniques. Meditation is a perceived rather than intellectual experience, making it highly subjective. Achieving states of meditation is an ongoing, layered process, much like peeling an onion. With continued practice, you will discover deeper layers of the onion.

Approach meditation without expectations of success or failure. This will allow you to be open to the experience at hand. Maintain a positive, open mind. To reap a beautiful harvest, plant your mind with a good CROP by being Curious, Relaxed, Open, and Patient in your attitude.

Throughout the book, dots (...) in the meditation sequences indicate that you should pause.

Basic Sitting Postures

To begin practicing meditation, choose a formal position that you find most comfortable. You do not have to be able to sit in a traditional Eastern posture. It is more important that you discover a position for your body that allows you to relax and be comfortable. Whether you choose to sit in a chair or on a mat on the floor, correct posture will allow the universal energy to flow properly through the head, hands, feet, and along the spine.

Modified Egyptian Pose

The ancient Egyptians meditated in an upright position as if they were sitting in a straight-backed chair. The practitioner might sit on a rock with their feet on the ground, hands resting in the lap, eyes open and fixated on a spot in front of his or her body.

A modified Egyptian pose can be most comfortable since it allows the spine to be straight and supported. It is important that you maintain good posture while sitting. This opens the diaphragm, allowing for proper breath flow and enhancing the flow of chi along the energy centers of the spine.

Choose a straight-backed chair to sit in. Sit with your back straight and your feet planted on the floor about hip-distance apart. Gently roll your shoulders back and down. This will lift and slightly open your chest, allowing your energy to be receptive. Rest your hands gently in your lap with the palms facing upward. The open-hand position symbolizes openness and creates a pathway for the healing energy to flow down the arms and out into the aura (the human energy field). Keep your head upright while tilting your chin slightly forward to create a clear air passage. Close your eyes softly.

Floor Positions

Traditional Eastern sitting poses do not provide back support. The practitioner sits on a cushion such as a zafu. If you need back support, try a meditation chair called a Back Jack. The chair allows you to sit on a cushion on the floor but has a built-in back support. You may purchase this type of chair on the Internet, at local health food stores, or yoga supply stores.

If you are able to sit on the floor without back support, you will need a mat or cushion to soften your contact with the floor. Experiment with different postures to determine which is most comfortable for you. The following are the most popular postures for Westerners.

Heels Together

Sit on your mat with legs slightly crossed but not folded under one another. Place one heel against the other so that the right and left heels align. This alignment will direct energy toward the root

energy center (chakra) at the base of the spine. The root center provides the base of the body's energy system and is the foundation that promotes wellness.

Japanese Style

Sit on a firm cushion with your heels resting under your buttocks. This creates a strong base for balance, although it can put a strain on the knees.

Cross-legged

Simply sit on the cushion with your legs crossed one over the other. If your hips are tight, you may prefer to sit on an extra towel propped under the buttocks. This will tip your sacrum forward slightly, encouraging a continuous line along the back. Rest your hands in a cupped position on your lap or place your palms facing upward on your knees.

Hand Positions

Throughout the ages, the hands have been used to pray and symbolize communication with a higher or cosmic power. Hand positions in meditation represent different meanings and play an important role in assisting healing. The hands may be seen as symbolizing the inner self and as a way to connect to the universal energy flow. In Western traditions, we are most familiar with the prayer position where the palms of both hands are pressed together and fingers point upward.

Try experimenting with different hand positions to find the one that works best for you.

Open Palms

This position symbolizes openness and creates a pathway for the healing energy to flow down the arms and out into the aura (the human energy field). Allow the hands to be relaxed and to rest gently on the lap or on the knees with palms facing upward.

Cupped Hands (Gesture of Meditation or Dhyana Mudra)

The right hand represents the yang quality of the masculine and the mind. The left represents the yin quality of the feminine and the heart. The right hand rests in the open palm of the left to represent the mind bowing to the wisdom of the heart. The hands form a circle. This position is commonly used in Buddhist meditation to symbolize the mind in a calm and concentrated state.

Mudra of Knowledge (Gyana Mudra)

Buddhist and Hindu yoga traditions utilize a sacred sign language to communicate different intentions during meditation or sacred dance. These sacred hand positions are called *mudras* (pronounced moo-dras). A mudra can be done with one or both hands. The mudra helps to seal the practitioner's energy into a concentrated state.

The most commonly used hand position in meditation in general is called the Gyana mudra. The forefinger and thumb of each hand close together, forming an energy seal that symbolizes wholeness (see below).

To form the receptive Gyana mudra, the thumb must be tucked under the forefinger. The receptive Gyana mudra symbol represents "inviting the teacher" and is used to invite the healer that lies within. It signifies the joining of individual and cosmic consciousness. The circle created by the fingers touching represents "birth," symbolizing the seeking of knowledge and new consciousness.

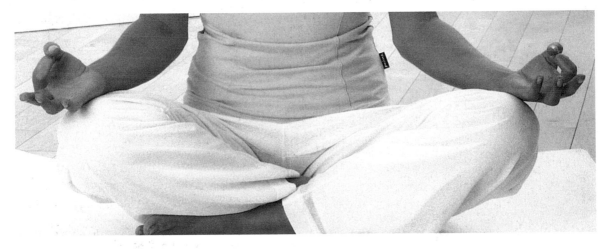

Basic Breathing

Focusing the breath is a universal and essential element to successful visualization and meditation practice. The word "breath" comes from the Greek word *psyche pneuma*, meaning breath, soul, air, and the vital spirit. Breathing is vital to our very existence and intricately connected to our health and wellness. Many people, however, are unaware of the importance of proper breathing and take it for granted. Under the demands of fast-paced schedules, we develop poor breathing patterns and take shallow and incomplete breaths. Breath restriction greatly diminishes the flow of vital energy that is central to health and wellness.

Conscious breathing is a tremendous resource for renewing and enhancing vital energy. Breathing is the primary means for gathering and utilizing the vital force of chi within the body. An unimpeded flow of energy promotes relaxation, an abundant supply of oxygen, and alert thinking. Learning basic breath control helps to still and focus the mind. The breath can be used as the practice itself (called mindfulness meditation) or within the meditation technique.

Counting the Breath

In this exercise, you simply observe the inhalation and exhalation of your breath. You will then add a pause between the inhalation and exhalation, divide the breath in thirds, and finally create a counting rhythm. You may sit in a chair or cross-legged on the floor with your back supported.

In time, you may wish to increase the count to eight on the inhalation and hold for a count of four (step 8).

1 Choose a seated posture on the floor or in a chair. Sit with a straight back and the palms of the hands resting upward on your lap. Take a moment to get comfortable...Close your eyes... Place your tongue on the roof of your mouth... Take a few slow, gentle breaths.

2 Focus your attention on the tip of your nostrils and feel the sensations of the breath entering and leaving the nose...As you breathe, feel the stomach rise and fall as the air fills the lower halves of your lungs...Follow as the chest rises and the air reaches the upper lungs...Notice the natural rhythm of the breath...Observe the full duration of your inhalation and exhalation. Keep your breathing smooth and regular.

3 Take a deep inhalation, then exhale slowly, allowing the shoulders to relax and drop down. Repeat. Take another deep breath, then exhale slowly, releasing any tension from the upper back...

4 With your next inhalation, imagine you are gathering the universal chi into the top of your head...As you exhale, imagine distributing the chi into every cell of your body. If your mind begins to wander, simply redirect it to the breath...

5 Observe the breath as it flows into its full capacity...Now watch as the breath flows fully out of the body. The breath flows in; the breath flows out...Simply watch and observe...

6 Now add a pause to the breath. Draw the breath in to its full capacity and pause... Release the exhalation fully...Now pause...Watch the breath flow in, pause...The breath flows out, and pause...The breath flows in, pause...The breath flows out, pause.

7 Now divide the breath into thirds. Breathe in to a third of your capacity, pause for a count of one...Breathe in another third, pause for a count of one...Breathe in one last time and pause...Now reverse by breathing out a third and pausing for a count of one...Breathe out another third, pause for a count of one...Breathe all the way out. Continue this "breathing in thirds" for several rounds until you become comfortable with the rhythm. Remember, if the mind wanders or you lose track, simply begin again.

8 Now shift your focus to inhale to a count of four and hold for a count of two...Exhale for four and hold for two...Inhale for four...hold for two...Exhale for four...hold for two.

9 Continue following this pattern for several minutes. When you are ready, release your counting and return your attention to the simple inhalation and exhalation of your breath...Open your eyes and take a moment to readjust.

Observing the Breath

In mindful meditation, you focus your mind on the breath. This trains the mind to experience the present moment. This discipline can greatly enhance the mind/body connection.

You can practice mindfulness both during meditation and at other times. One way to practice is to become aware of the breath throughout the day. Take the time to stop at different points during the day to notice your breath. Observing how you are breathing will quite naturally teach you about your changing emotional and mental states. Learning your breath patterns is simply a matter of reminding yourself to pay attention. Over time, you will become more attuned to your emotions and thoughts and will be able to respond to stress with a relaxed and full breathing pattern.

When we are feeling stressed or experiencing "negative" thoughts or emotions, it is quite usual to take short, shallow, or rapid breaths. Often we have a tendency to hold our breath. However, it is during the experience of stress that you can benefit the most by directing the breath to slow down and become full. As the breath begins to calm and regulate itself, you will notice that the body can process the emotional and mental changes of the current situation. When you find yourself in a state of excitement, frustration, impatience, confusion, or anxiety, simply stop and notice the breath. The simple act of noticing will begin to shift the breath. The challenge here is to be able to actually catch yourself "in the act."

1 Begin by choosing a comfortable position. Close your eyes...Place your tongue on the ridge behind your upper teeth...Take in a few slow, gentle breaths. Release any need to control your breath. The intention is to discover and reveal your natural breath, the way you used to breathe before any poor habits were formed.

2 Adopt an inquisitive attitude toward your breath. In what areas of your body do you notice the breath?...Can you feel the breath expanding your rib cage?...How far does your breath reach into your body?...Does it flow freely through your throat?...

Does the breath come to rest high up in the shoulder area or the upper chest?...Does it reach down to the abdomen?...Can you feel the gentle rise and fall of the abdomen?

3 Continue your investigation. How would you describe the qualities of your breath pattern? Does it feel smooth or rough?...Does it seem even?...Is your breath shallow or fast? (Be patient, as your first perceptions may provide generalized rather than specific information.)

4 Watch the inhalation of the breath for a few moments without trying to change it. Do not be concerned with whether you are breathing "properly." Simply observe without evaluation and allow your breathing to be smooth and regular.

5 Now direct your attention to the natural pause between the inhalation and the exhalation of your breath. How do you phrase your breath?... Do you notice any marked difference between the inhalation and exhalation?...Do they seem equal in length?

6 Notice that at the end of the inhalation you experience the "top" of the breath. As you exhale fully at the end of the exhalation, you experience the "bottom" of the breath.

7 In the pauses at the top and bottom of the breath, the body experiences complete rest. Take a moment to notice these resting pauses.

8 Imagine that the duration between the "top" and the "bottom" of the breath flows so that the breath stretches out to feel circular and without beginning or end. Surrender into the ongoing ebb and flow of your breath.

9 When you feel ready, let go of any images you are working with...Take a long, deep, full breath...Remember what your external surroundings look like and gently open your eyes.

Abdominal Breathing

Breathing from the abdomen or diaphragm strongly enhances the mind/body connection and reduces tension caused by stress. When you breathe with your abdomen it is difficult to be tense at the same time. You breathe more deeply and fully when you are relaxed. If you watch infants breathe, you will see that they breathe from their abdomen, as this is our natural breathing pattern. As we mature, however, we tend to adopt poor breathing patterns that can add to stressful reactions. Teaching yourself to use abdominal breathing will promote a state of calm and serenity.

1 Begin by lying on your back with your legs straight or bent at the knee and your feet flat on the floor. Allow the weight of your back and buttocks to settle gently into the floor. Close your eyes...Place your tongue on the roof of your mouth...Take a few deep, cleansing breaths.

2 Place the palms of your hands on your abdomen, the region below the sternum and above the pubic bone...Feel the weight of your hands resting on your belly...

3 Begin a gentle observation...Are you holding any tension in the belly?...Notice how the abdomen moves with each inhalation and

exhalation...Feel how it swells and settles like a balloon inflating and deflating...On the in-breath, notice how the abdomen swells out, up, to the sides and into the lower back...The abdomen settles back gently without constriction or tension on the out-breath.

4 Each breath flows naturally and with a gentle fullness...Visualize a bright white light above your head. This light is the energy of the heaven chi...Draw this chi in through the top of your head and direct it to the reservoir of the lower abdomen.

5 The belly becomes soft and expansive, filling with heaven chi...Your abdomen becomes a beach ball that inflates slightly larger with each inhalation and exhalation...The ball enlarges, yet remains soft and pliable...The abdomen softens to allow space for the large, round ball...Imagine your beach ball floating gently on the swells of a great lake...The ball rises and falls with each swell of the breath.

6 Follow the rhythm of the beach ball rising and falling until you have achieved your desired level of expansion and relaxation of the abdomen...When you are ready, open your eyes and return your attention to your external surroundings.

Basic Techniques
Grounding, Rooted Feet

The concept of grounding is important to meditation practice and healing. Grounding is a way to center yourself and release excess energy accumulated by stress and tension.

To "ground" essentially means to make an energetic connection between your body and the earth. Being grounded is the sensation of feeling connected to your inner self and anchored with the earth. You already have natural ways to make yourself feel grounded, such as cooking, gardening, eating, exercising, conversing with a friend, or enjoying the solitude of silence.

Grounding enables you to train your body to "let go" of tension. Everyday tension can create undue physical, emotional, and mental distress and fatigue. Think of your physical body as a beautiful vase filled with life force. Daily stress contaminates your life force, turning it into dirty, cloudy water. The tool of grounding helps you empty the vase of excessive energy and replenish your life force with creativity. And, like an underground spring continually moving, the water in your vase circulates, remaining clear and pristine.

The following grounding technique will help you train yourself to "let go" throughout the day, rather than allowing tension and stress to build up.

1 Choose a straight-backed chair for this exercise. This will allow your feet to be planted solidly on the floor. Lean forward slightly so your spine is straight but relaxed. Close your eyes... Place your tongue on the roof of your mouth and take a few slow, deep breaths, feeling your lungs fill with fresh oxygen...Focus on this intake and distribution of oxygen several times until you feel sufficiently relaxed.

2 On the next inhalation, envisage a brilliant point of golden light, 12 inches (30 cm) or so above your head. This point of light is the universal life force shining down upon you. Imagine the light intensifying as you focus upon it...With the in-breath, draw this light down through the top of your head and into your body.

3 The golden light travels through your body from head to toe. As this cosmic force enters your body, picture it creating an axis of light. The axis runs from the top of your head down through your body and out through your feet. It then continues down to the core of the earth and back out into the universe.

4 Focus on the vital cosmic energy moving through your center from head to toe...
On your next exhalation, picture the light being

exhaled downward through your legs and out through the soles of your feet...As you exhale, the light roots of energy extend from the bottom of your feet, reaching downward into the earth.

5 These roots become the grounding connection that enables you to drain tension or excessive energy from your body...With each inhalation and exhalation, the roots reach further and further into the earth until you feel a strong, secure connection.

6 Feel your feet becoming increasingly heavy and warm. Feel your entire body beginning to feel heavy and warm, solid and weighted...Breathe into this sensation of heaviness and warmth...

7 Starting at the top of your head, make a large mental sweep of your body...Notice if you are holding tension or tightness in your scalp, facial muscles, jaw, or neck...Any tension or discomfort gathers into a mist...

8 Direct the mist to flow out of your body and drain through the roots extending from the bottom of your feet...The soil of the earth soaks up this mist and recycles it into pure energy.

9 Return your attention to your upper torso, scanning for tension in the shoulders and upper chest...The tension gathers into a mist...Release this mist through the body and out through the soles of your feet.

10 Relax into the sensations of being grounded and connected to the earth. Continue the scan in the upper torso, seeking tension or tightness in the upper back, arms and hands, and midchest...Imagine tension and tightness turning into mist...Release this vapor down through your body and out through the soles of your feet...Repeat this scan for your abdomen, lower back, buttocks, and legs, each time gathering the mist and instructing it to drain through the roots of your feet.

11 When you are ready, return your attention to the simple inhalation and exhalation of the breath. Try to maintain the sense of grounding as you slowly open your eyes and readjust to your surroundings.

The Observer

Cultivating an attitude of observation is fundamental to meditation practice. By learning to observe, the mind is able to detach while allowing you to remain alert and receptive. The mind is trained to observe without reacting with judgment or evaluation. You can learn to observe your thoughts as well as your emotional states and physical sensations. You can then experience your inner world and the world around you free from attachment. This process allows you to remain calm, regardless of the weather of the mind. The aspect of the mind that develops this unfolding ability to observe is often referred to as the "observer" or the "witness consciousness."

A common misperception is that meditation requires you to be able to control the mind. The Zen Buddhist tradition teaches that to attempt to control the mind is a fruitless endeavor. Rather than try to control the mind, you can learn to assign it new tasks.

The mind can be compared to a river that is continuously flowing. Thoughts are carried along the currents of the mind. Therefore, to "think" is to do what comes naturally to the mind. Rather than try to control your thoughts, you can learn to develop a new relationship to them. By learning to watch your river of thoughts, you learn to break free from conditioned responses. And, contrary to what one might expect, by learning detachment you are able to experience life more fully because the filters of the mind no longer bind you.

Key words that may help to convey the quality of observation are to watch, notice, detect, discover, recognize, and perceive.

1 For this exercise, sit in a chair or your preferred position on the floor. Take a few moments to get comfortable. Close your eyes...Place your tongue on the roof of your mouth...Take a few slow, gentle breaths...Each time you exhale, let any tension from the activities of the day melt away...Notice the natural rhythm of the breath and follow the path of the inhalation and exhalation. With each breath, feel more attentive and present within this very moment.

2 Direct your attention to a quiet place deep within, a place you are naturally drawn to when seeking solace. This may be a place within your body or your mind. It is a place of calm reflection. Here you will find a part of yourself that has recorded all the significant and subtle details of daily life. This part of the self is the "observer." The observer is able to witness sensations, emotions, thoughts, and events without judgment.

3 Begin to work with the inner observer by watching the breath. Allow the breath to come naturally and with a gentle evenness. Notice that it is not necessary to do any extra work. The body knows how to breathe on its own.

4 In your mind's eye, "watch" the rise and fall of your stomach...Observe your inhalation and the natural cycle of the breath as you follow with the exhalation...Notice how the act of consciously observing the breath changes your relationship to the breath...With each inhalation and exhalation,

notice the sensations that come and go. The breath creates space for all that arises without fear or resistance.

5 Now turn your attention to your mind. Your mind may be engaged with distractions. In fact, your attention may be in several different places at once. Do not judge or evaluate. There is no need to make any changes. Simply observe with interest and kind attention.

6 Your mind becomes a vast blue sky...Thoughts appear as clouds of different sizes, shapes, and textures. Watch as the clouds drift by across the sky. As the clouds come and go, the thoughts continuously arise and disappear...Let go of any desire to grasp onto a passing thought. As the clouds move by, begin to sense a feeling of timelessness. There is nothing to accomplish in this moment, nothing to do except receive the breath and watch the thoughts drift by.

7 When you feel ready, return your attention to your body. Remember what your external surroundings look like and gently open your eyes. When the chakras (see "Vital Centers of the Body") spin in proper balance, each energy center contributes to the overall health of the body by equalizing the nervous and endocrine systems. Stress and worry can negatively impact this balance. Regular meditation can counter this negative influence by balancing the chakras. In the following visualization, we will cleanse and clear each center.

Chakra Cleansing and Balancing

1 Choose a comfortable position...Close your eyes...Place your tongue on the roof of your mouth and begin focusing on your breath. As your mind feels clear and your body relaxed, turn your attention to the earth energy below you.

2 Take a moment to make a grounding connection with your feet to the energy of the earth...Feel your feet become heavy and warm... Feel any tension releasing from your body to drain out through the bottom of the feet...Imagine the soil of the earth soaking up the energy of the tension and recycling it into pure energy.

3 Just as the earth is the solid foundation we walk upon, so the first chakra is the foundation of our energy system. We will begin cleansing the first center. Direct your attention to this center, located at the base of the spine.

4 Breathe into the center and feel the force of gravity gently acting upon this first chakra... The gravity activates this center as it begins to spin counterclockwise or clockwise (whichever direction feels appropriate). The spinning of the chakra releases excessive energy or blocks to your physical well-being.

5 Imagine that a heavenly sea of chi (universal energy) surrounds you...The essence of the sea laps into your body and recedes...The sea flows into your body and ebbs out...Focus on this rhythm of ebb and flow...

6 Now focus the waves of the sea to the first chakra...As the waves flow in the chi, stimulating the center with vitality, the center begins to unfold like the petals of a flower...The chi fills the petals with a reddish brown color...The vibrant color radiates out into the base of the spine.

7 Move your attention to the sacral center, the second chakra located between the navel and pubic bone...Again tap into the sensations of this sea of chi surrounding you...The chi circulates into the sacral area, the center of sexual and creative energy...Watch as the sea flows into the center...a flower appears and begins to unfold to reveal petals of vivid orange...The orange petals begin to spin and balance the chakra...See the color radiating into the lower abdomen and lower back...

8 Imagine the sea of chi lapping into the third chakra at the solar plexus, which houses emotional and personal power...Feel the waves of the sea ebb and flow at the solar plexus...The vitality of the chi fills this center with a bright yellow color... The petals of this flower begin to unfold and radiate its color into the stomach...The spinning petals release any tightness or tension you hold in the stomach...As the chakra spins, the emotional body is cleansed...

9 Turn your attention to the heart center in the middle of your chest...The sea flows into this center, bringing gentle cleansing and refreshment... The flower petals unfold to reveal a brilliant green that radiates out into the chest...The heart is the center of affinity and the bridge of transformation between the physical and spiritual domains. The green color of the heart symbolizes nature, growth, and harmony. The green creates harmony between the lower and upper chakras...As the green radiates into the body, the heart center extends compassion to all living things...

10 Direct your attention now to the fifth center, located at the throat, the center of creative expression, pragmatic intuition, and higher will... The waves lap into this center, causing the petals to spin and revitalize...The petals vibrate as an electric blue...This blue reflects clarity of the higher mind... The ebb and flow of the universal chi cleanses this center, bringing a sense of clarity for self-expression.

11 Move your attention upward to the brow center, located between your eyes. The sea flows in and out of the sixth chakra...Feel the vital chi stimulating the opening of the flower...The petals unveil a lovely indigo color that awakens the center of clairvoyance and imagination...As the indigo flows outward, the higher qualities of intuition are released to offer guidance to your life.

12 Finally, direct your attention to the point at the crown of the head...This is the flower with a thousand petals...As the sea of chi flows and ebbs, this supreme center is activated, spilling forth a brilliant white light tinged with violet purple...This is the center of cosmic consciousness that promotes the ability to achieve atonement or "at-one-ment"

with the cosmic power...It is the center of highest consciousness. Visualize the opening of this flower... Its radiant light bathes your entire body with replenishing chi.

13 Now slowly reverse down the spine, gently closing the petals of each flower, starting at the crown center and working down to the root...Return your attention to the flow of the breath...When you are ready, slowly return to a waking state and give yourself time to readjust to your surroundings.

Therapeutic Techniques

Concentration and Focus

The following treatments are helpful in developing concentration and focus:

a) Focusing on an Object

b) Center of Head

Focusing on an Object

Origin: A basic beginning meditation practice found in various Eastern traditions.

🕴 **Objective: To cultivate concentration and focus**

🔄 **Frequency of use: May be used once or twice daily**

🕐 **Duration: Sustain meditation for 10–15 minutes**

↔ **Cross-reference: Use Observing the Breath (page 28)**

① **Difficulty level 1: Easily executed**

🌿 **Complementary treatment: Observing the Breath (page 28)**

⊕ **Quick remedy**

A simple way to learn concentration and centering is by training the mind to focus on an object. Try a simple object such as a candle flame, an apple, or a bowl. Place the object on a plain surface about 20 inches (50 cm) below eye level. Begin by focusing on the object with your eyes open, then with your eyes closed.

If this is the first time you are doing this exercise, select an apple to focus on. From then on, practice focusing on different types of still objects.

1 Sit in a straight-backed chair. Place the apple on a plain, clear surface arm's length in front of you, about 20 inches (50 cm) below eye level.

2 Close your eyes...Place your tongue on the roof of your mouth...Begin by Observing the Breath...When you feel sufficiently relaxed, open your eyes and begin to gaze at the apple. Bring the apple into focus, allowing everything else to become part of the background.

3 Trace the contours of the apple with your eyes...Notice with great detail its shape and texture. Breathe in its color...Imagine holding the apple...Imagine biting into the apple...Feel the juiciness and taste its sweetness. Imagine all the sensations you would experience by chewing the apple.

4 Now see the apple as whole once again. With your mind's eye, make an impression of the apple, like a camera capturing an image on film...Close your eyes and take time to recreate the picture of the apple in your mind.

5 See the size and shape of the apple...Picture its vivid color and the texture of the skin. Smell the apple...Imagine biting into it and the taste filling your mouth. If your mind begins to wander or you lose the picture of the apple, simply open your eyes and look again at its features. Repeat this until you feel confident holding the image of the apple in your mind.

6 Return your focus to the simple inhalation and exhalation of the breath...Focus on the breath for a few cycles...When you feel ready, slowly open your eyes.

Center of Head

Origin: Based on Hindu practices utilizing the chakra system, this meditation fosters concentration and objectivity.

Objective: **To cultivate clarity, concentration, and focus**

Frequency of use: **May be used on a daily basis**

Duration: **Sustain meditation for 10–15 minutes**

Cross-reference: **Use Observing the Breath (page 28)**

Difficulty level 2: **Try this exercise subsequent to Focusing on an Object (page 38)**

Complementary treatment: **The Observer (page 32)**

When you have developed sufficient focus, you may choose to use the brow center as your center for all meditation practice.

1 Choose a seated posture from Basic Sitting Postures (page 20)...Close your eyes...and engage in Observing the Breath.

2 Imagine an energetic ball of light glowing at your tailbone. Move the ball of energy upward to the region of your lower belly, 2 or 3 inches (5–7 cm) below the navel...Take a few breaths...Notice any sensations...Move the ball up to your solar plexus and breathe deeply...Notice any sensations at the solar plexus...Move the energy ball up to your heart center, located at the sternum...Notice what it feels like to center your awareness here...Move the ball upward to your throat center at the soft space between the clavicle bones...Notice the perspective of centering here...Finally, move the ball of energy up into your brow center, behind the eyes and between your ears.

3 Allow the ball to come to rest here...This is the center of your head, the central place of awareness...Breathe and focus on the ball of light...Does this center have a different feeling or quality from the others?...The center of the head is the place from which to observe all that you experience within and around you, without judgment or evaluation. Here you can experience a detached overview from your thoughts and sensations that arise.

4 The ball of energy becomes a bright blue light...The blue light expands throughout your head, radiating mental clarity...The luminosity radiates beyond your head, out into the space around you...Ripples of light move into your aura like ripples on a pond moving ever outward. This blue light expands its radius further and further with each breath...

5 The definition of your physical body begins to soften and dissolve as you melt into the blue expansiveness...This mental clarity brings awareness of all you are experiencing physically, emotionally, and mentally...

6 Retract the radiant blue light by pulling it closer to your body, like wrapping yourself in a blanket...Let go of the image of the light... Gently return your attention to the inhalation and exhalation of the breath. Bring yourself to waking consciousness by counting backward from ten to one, then open your eyes.

Centering and Inner Balance

The following treatments promote centering and inner balance:

a) Grounding Cord   b) Offering the Colors   c) Garden Sanctuary

Grounding Cord

Origin: A common meditation found in shamanic practices and ancient European traditions.

🧍 **Objection: To create centering and inner balance**

🌀 **Frequency of use: May be used on a daily basis**

◉ **Duration: Sustain meditation for 10–15 minutes**

↔ **Cross-reference: Use Observing the Breath (page 28)**

① **Difficulty level 1: Use this technique as a daily practice**

✎ **Complementary treatments: Center of Head (page 40) and Mental Sponge (page 61)**

✚ **Quick remedy: Once you are familiar with this technique it can be considered a quick remedy**

1 Choose your preferred meditation position. Close your eyes...Place your tongue on the roof of your mouth...Hands are relaxed and open, resting on your lap. Engage in Observing the Breath ...With each breath, feel your body becoming increasingly heavy, warm, and relaxed.

2 Direct your attention to your tailbone... The breath gathers like a pool of water at the base of your spine. Imagine your favorite tree. The branches and leaves of the tree wrap around your tailbone, creating the sense that you are part of the tree...Imagine being a child...Climb up and nestle in the arms of the tree. Your breath flows into the branches and extends out to the leaves. The tree trunk is hollow...Extend it down through the many layers of the earth's soil and rock...The trunk stays hollow as it descends all the way to the very core of the earth. Follow your breath all the way down to the hot, molten core.

3 The tree trunk reaches the center...As you connect to this powerful source of gravity, feel the weight and heaviness of your body increasing... The roots of the tree trunk wrap firmly and securely around the center of the earth.

4 The hollow trunk is your grounding cord. The connection to the earth acts as a giant vacuum to help you release any sensations, feelings, or thoughts that you no longer need to hold on to.

5 Redirect your attention to your body. Do a mental sweep, searching for pain, discomfort, or concerns that you are ready to release...What you choose to release becomes a smokelike energy... See this energy release down your grounding cord like water draining from a bathtub...Repeat this mental sweep several times until you feel cleansed and ready to move on.

6 Whenever you release energy, it is important to replenish. Imagine a bright, golden sun, 10 or 12 inches (25–30 cm) above your head. Draw this gold sun into your body, instructing it to replenish any places where energy was released...When you feel as if you have soaked up as much golden energy as possible, take a few deep breaths and gently open your eyes.

Your grounding cord can be made out of any material you like. The cord helps you release any negative or excessive energy so that you do not become overly saturated and imbalanced.

Offering the Colors

Origin: A simple yet beautiful meditation technique originating from the Tantric tradition.

- Objective: To achieve mental clarity

- Frequency of use: May be used on a regular basis

- Duration: Sustain meditation for 5–10 minutes

- Cross-reference: Use Observing the Breath (page 28) and Cupped Hands (page 25)

- Difficulty level 1: A simple technique that requires some practice

- Complementary treatment: Center of Head (page 40)

- Quick remedy

Offering the Colors is a meditation that arises from the Tantric yoga tradition. It encourages us to release our thoughts to a greater universal mind.

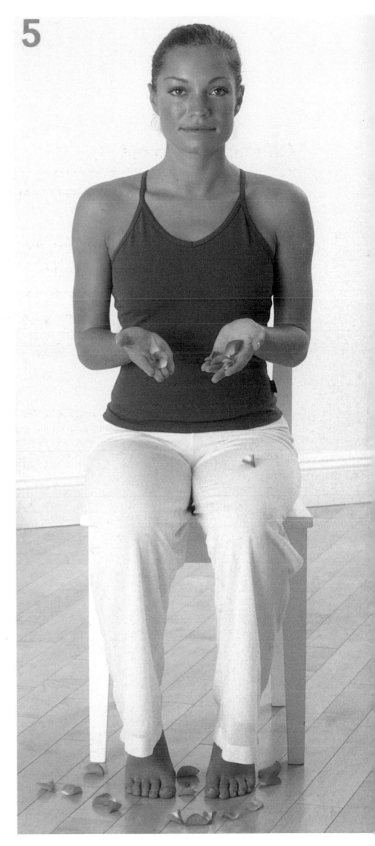

1 Begin in a seated position of your choice...
Close your eyes and engage in Breath
Focusing...Breathe deeply to allow the chi,
the universal life force, to enter your body.

2 When you feel sufficiently relaxed, turn your
attention to your mind...Be aware of the
ways in which your mind may be distracted.
Do not judge this but simply observe. The mind
and spirit have the ability to be in more than one
place at a time. This quality is not something that
requires controlling; instead it may be considered
a spiritual ability. Simply having awareness of the
ways in which the mind becomes distracted raises
your consciousness.

3 Place your attention on your thoughts. Visualize
the thoughts as colors...Your intuition guides
you in assigning colors to these thoughts...Breathe
into these thoughts...See them turning into different
colors of the spectrum.

4 Now cup your hands and place them level with
the heart center at the sternum. See the colors
of your thoughts turning into beautiful flowers and
cascading into your cupped palms...Breathe the
fullness of this bouquet into the heart center while
surrendering any attachment or responsibility toward
these thoughts.

5 Open the hands and drop them to the sides
of your body. See the flowers releasing into the
earth where Mother Earth graciously accepts them.
Offer the colors to the earth, quietly surrendering
your thoughts to the wisdom of the greater mind.

6 Repeat this sequence as many times as you like
to clear the mind. Return your attention to the
breath and then to your external surroundings.

Garden Sanctuary

Origin: Western; a guided imagery technique in which the participant experiences an inner virtual reality to gain a sense of center, rejuvenation, and inner balance.

Objective: To create an inner sanctuary for a calm, peaceful mind

Frequency of use: May be used on a daily basis

Duration: Sustain meditation for as long as you wish

Cross-reference: Use Abdominal Breathing (page 29) and Mudra of Knowledge (page 25)

Difficulty level 2: Requires ability to sustain concentration

Complementary treatment: Center of Head (page 40)

1 Choose a comfortable position...Close your eyes and engage in Abdominal Breathing... The breath becomes a light breeze that gently lifts you and takes you to the entrance of a special garden...Walk through the gates of the garden, feeling the senses of your body awaken...Here in this sanctuary you have an enchanting ability to create or change any details you wish.

2 Your eyes sweep across the garden bathed in splendid colors. Soak in all the delightful sights... What does your garden look like? Is it a whimsical patchwork of color or is it a formal design?...Notice the variety of flora growing throughout the garden... Perhaps you see some of your favorites? What fauna do you see out enjoying the day?

3 Take a deep breath, enjoying the fragrance of the garden's aromas...Can you distinguish any particular aromas?...Perhaps you can hear the sound of buzzing insects and singing birds?

4 Find yourself drawn to a particular section of the garden. Reach out and caress the foliage or petals of the plants and flowers. Marvel at the variety of textures at your fingertips.

5 Continue to stroll through the garden, feeling the earth beneath your feet, or select an area of the garden to sit in and rest...Remember, you can control the weather and temperature...Again, breathe in the sights with all your senses...Notice the interplay of light in the garden...Is it a bright, sunny day or partly cloudy? Notice the sensation of warmth on your skin from the sun, or perhaps moisture from a cooling mist or rain...Enjoy your garden sanctuary as long as you like...

6 At your leisure, leave the garden with one last glance...Take a moment to savor your experience...Slowly return your attention to your entire body...Give yourself the suggestion that, as you return to waking consciousness, you will feel refreshed and revitalized. Focus again on the gentle rhythm of the breath...When you are ready, open your eyes.

Stress and Tension

The following treatments are excellent for releasing stress and tension:

a) Gold Ball Scan   b) PMR—Progressive Muscle Relaxation

Gold Ball Scan

Origin: Based on a combination of Eastern and Western practices utilizing the energy of light for inner healing.

Objective: Relaxation for the entire body

Frequency of use: May be used on a regular basis

Duration: Sustain practice for 10–15 minutes

Cross-reference: Use Abdominal Breathing (page 29) and Open Palms (page 24)

Difficulty level 1: Requires simple imagery

Complementary treatment: Progressive Muscle Relaxation (page 46)

Quick remedy

1 Begin in a comfortable lying-down or reclining position. Close your eyes...Engage in Abdominal Breathing.

2 Visualize a vibrant golden ball of energy floating directly above your head...With your breath, move this ball downward across your forehead...The heat of the ball relaxes the muscles of the forehead.

3 The golden ball washes across your eyes, removing tension or tightness. The ball rolls down across your cheeks, mouth, and jaw muscles, melting away any tension. The heat and light of the ball penetrates the skin, creating deeper relaxation.

4 The energy ball continues to flow downward, moving across your throat to the front of your shoulders, melting away stress.

5 Focus on the movement of the ball as it rolls across your chest. Feel relaxation and warmth spreading across your chest, down into your arms, and out through your hands.

6 Move the gold ball down into your abdomen, pubic bone, and groin area, feeling the warmth melting away any tightness.

7 The energy ball continues along the tops of your thighs and calves, descending all the way to your toes and feet. The gold ball rolls to the back of your body...Starting at the soles, it moves upward.

8 Systematically move this ball up the back of your body, touching the same areas as before.

9 As you become familiar with this pattern, you may be able to move the energy ball quickly through several cycles until you achieve the desired level of relaxation.

PMR—Progressive Muscle Relaxation

Origin: A technique that systematically relaxes all the muscles of the body. Dr. Edmund Jacobsen developed this method of relaxation in the 1920s as part of a training program in instructing individuals how to use the mind to achieve deep relaxation.

Objective: Relaxation for the entire body

Frequency of use: May be used on a regular basis

Duration: Sustain practice for 15–20 minutes

Cross-reference: Use Open Palms (page 24) and Concentration and Focus (page 88)

Difficulty level 1: Easy-to-follow, step-by-step instructions

Complementary treatment: Autogenic Training (page 54)

Quick remedy

This technique systematically relaxes all the muscles of the body. The goal of PMR is to eliminate residual tension in the body, thereby achieving a state of complete relaxation. Once you have become familiar with the relaxation sequence, you can easily do it in about 10 minutes.

1 Choose a comfortable position, either lying on your back or in a reclining position. Close your eyes...Place your tongue on the roof of your mouth and take three deep breaths, exhaling slowly each time.

2 Tighten your right foot by curling your toes downward...Hold for 8 seconds...Release and allow your muscles to go limp for 15 seconds.

3 Tighten your right lower leg by pulling your toes toward you and tightening your calf muscles. Hold for 8 seconds...Release and relax for 15 seconds.

4 Squeeze the muscles of your entire right leg by tightening your calf, thigh, hips, and buttocks. Hold...Release all the muscles and allow your right leg to go limp for 15 seconds.

5 Follow the same sequence for the left foot and leg.

6 Clench your right hand into a fist. Hold... and relax.

7 Tighten your right forearm and make a fist with your right hand. Hold and relax.

8 Squeeze your entire right arm, tightening your biceps by drawing your forearm up toward your shoulder and "making a muscle." Hold the tension for 8 seconds...Release and relax for 15 seconds.

9 Follow the same sequence for the left hand and arm.

10 Tighten your stomach muscles by drawing in your stomach. Hold and release...Feel a wave of relaxation move through your entire abdomen.

11 Tighten the muscles of your lower back by gently arching upward. (Omit this if you experience lower back pain.) Hold and release your back.

12 Constrict the muscles of your chest by drawing in a deep breath. Hold and release slowly. Imagine warmth expanding through your chest.

13 Carefully press your head into the floor to tighten the back of the neck. Hold...Release the weight of your head to a resting position. Take a deep breath and repeat. Draw your shoulder blades back as if you were going to make them touch. Hold for 8 seconds then relax for 15 seconds.

14 Tense the muscles of your forehead by raising your eyebrows as high as you can. Hold...and relax, feeling the muscles become smooth across the forehead.

15 Tense the muscles around your eyes by squeezing your eyelids tightly shut. Hold...Relax as the eye muscles go limp.

16 Tighten your jaw muscles by opening your mouth as widely as you can, stretching the muscles around the hinges of your jaw. Hold...Relax and let your lips part and the jaw hang loosely.

17 Scan your body for any residual tension. If any area remains tense, repeat a tensing cycling for that muscle group.

18 Feel a warm wave of relaxation spread throughout your body from toes to head. Gradually bring yourself to waking consciousness.

Back Pain

Consult a doctor before beginning meditative practice if your pain is a recent occurrence rather than a chronic condition. Be conservative in applying techniques and know your body's physical limits.

Consult a doctor if:
- The pain worsens during or after treatment.
- You experience sharp, shooting, or pinching pain during meditation.
- You experience muscle spasms.
- You experience pain radiating outward from the source.

The following treatments are excellent for thoracic (upper back) or lumbar (lower back) pain:
a) Passive Relaxation   b) Child's Pose   c) Down Dog Stretch

Passive Relaxation

Origin: Western; similar to Progressive Muscle Relaxation.

Objective: To treat pain in upper, middle, and lower back

Frequency of use: May be used on a daily basis

Duration: Hold the pose for 15–20 minutes

Cross-reference: Use Observing the Breath (page 28)

Difficulty level 1: Technique is easily carried out

Complementary treatments: Pain Release (page 59) and Color Release (page 58)

Quick remedy

1 Sit on the floor facing the front of a chair. Bring your hips and buttocks close to the front legs of the chair.

2 Place your calves onto the seat of the chair and slowly lower yourself onto your back.

3 Adjust your body so the edge of the chair seat is at the back of your knees. This allows the calf muscles to remain relaxed and passive.

4 Allow your arms to rest with the palms of the hands turned upward in a receiving position. (If this is uncomfortable for your neck, place a rolled-up towel under your neck.)

5 Gently close your eyes and take a few deep-cleansing breaths...

6 Give the weight of your body over to gravity. With each breath, feel yourself sinking deeply into the floor...Notice how your back is touching the floor...Do not force yourself to flatten out the lower back, but allow gravity time to encourage your back to relax gently. You are not doing the work; gravity is...

7 With your mind, follow the simple inhalation and exhalation of your breath. If your mind begins to wander, simply make a note of this and return your attention to the breath...

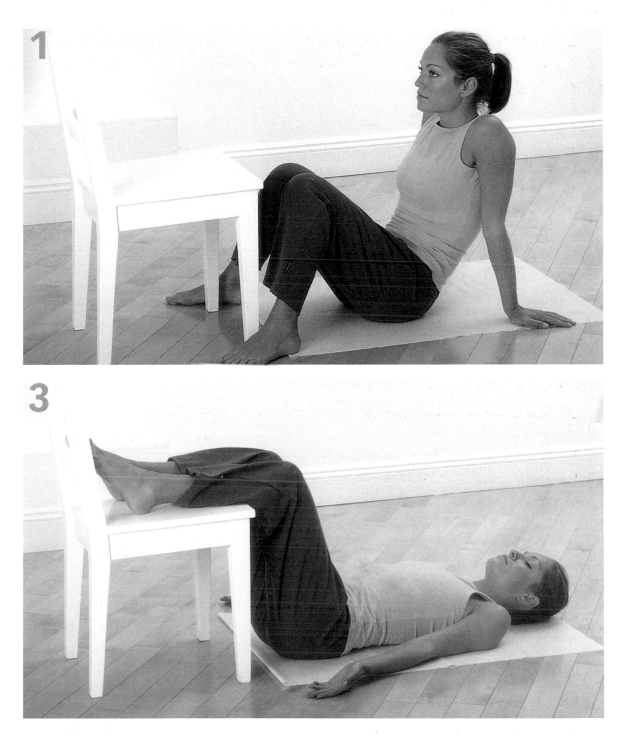

8 Hold this passive position for 15–20 minutes. If you are not achieving the results you seek, move on to another technique. When you are ready to finish the pose, gently lift your legs off the chair. Push back from the chair. Roll onto your right side and push yourself up with both hands into a sitting position.

Child's Pose

Origin: Various forms of Hatha yoga.

🏃 **Objective: To treat pain in lower back**

⏱ **Frequency of use: May be used on a daily basis, several times a day**

⏲ **Duration: Follow the technique for 5–10 minutes**

↔ **Cross-reference: Use Abdominal Breathing (page 29)**

① **Difficulty level 1**

🌿 **Complementary treatments: Counting the Breath (page 27) and Color Release (page 58)**

⊕ **Quick remedy**

This yoga technique is widely used as a resting/rejuvenating pose. It is highly effective for releasing pain in the lower back.

1 Begin this pose with a mat or towel under your body. You may need an extra hand towel for the forehead and/or knees (see photo).

2 Get onto your hands and knees with your hands shoulder-width apart and knees hip-width apart. (If this creates discomfort in your knees, place a folded towel under your kneecaps.)

3 Bring your big toes together and widen the stance of your knees and hips by a few inches, depending on your level of flexibility.

4 Slowly and gently begin to lower your buttocks to rest back onto your heels. At this point you may find you are able to widen your knees a bit further.

5 Begin to bend your elbows to touch the floor...Rest your forehead flat on the floor. You want the forehead to reach the floor. If it does not, or if the pressure is uncomfortable, place a towel or two beneath your forehead to provide support.

6 Sweep your right arm in an arc backward along the floor until it comes to rest behind your feet. Repeat with your left arm.

7 Turn the palms of your hands up, allowing your shoulders to roll forward and drop.

8 Close your eyes. Allow your belly to relax and drop downward toward the floor.

9 Follow the steps for Abdominal Breathing.

10 Hold the position for 5–10 minutes. When you feel ready, slowly lift your forehead and reverse the steps to come out of the pose.

Down Dog Stretch

Origin: Hatha and other yoga traditions. Excellent for releasing back pain while building flexibility and strength.

Ⓚ **Objective: To treat pain in lower, middle, and upper back**

Ⓢ **Frequency of use: Can be used once or twice daily**

Ⓓ **Duration: Begin by holding the position for one minute, then work up to three minutes with several repetitions**

Ⓐ **Cross-references: Use Abdominal Breathing (page 29) and Observing the Breath (page 28)**

① **Difficulty level 2: A comprehensive and advanced technique that requires strength, flexibility, and stamina**

Ⓒ **Complementary treatment: Child's Pose (page 50)**

Down Dog Stretch is a stretch for the whole spine. If you have extremely tight hamstrings or shoulders, you will not achieve back release. Instead, you may initially experience the stretch in the arms and backs of the legs. Over time, as these areas stretch out, you may eventually feel the stretch in the back.

This is an excellent pose for achieving back wellness and strength.

Go slowly when it is the first Down Dog Stretch of the day in order to allow your muscles to relax and soften.

1

First familiarize yourself with the mechanical sequence of getting into the Down Dog Stretch. When this is achieved, you are free to focus your attention on abdominal breathing throughout the pose. Focus your breath and breathe into any tightness or discomfort. Be careful not to hold the breath when your muscles feel challenged. Direct the breath to remain as steady and consistent as possible.

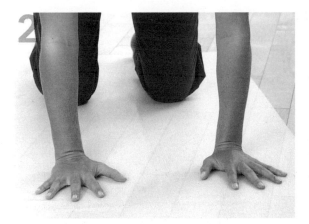

1 Position your body on your hands and knees with the hands shoulder-width apart and knees hip-width apart. If this creates discomfort in your knees, place a folded towel under them.

2 Spread your fingers wide apart and press the palms into the floor...Curl your toes under.

3 Shift your weight back into the legs as if you are beginning to squat. Keep your arms straight. Lift your knees off the ground, continuing to shift your weight back onto your feet.

4 Lift your knees until you achieve straight legs (you may wish to retain a soft bend in your knees). Move your hips backward as if someone had attached ropes to them and was gently pulling back and up. Keep your stomach firm (see illustration). At this point your position will resemble an upside-down "V."

5 Keep your arms straight and push away from the floor with your hands. Move your chest toward the thighs. Shift more of your weight into your legs while pressing your ankles toward the floor. The tailbone presses toward the back of the room. Your "V" shape will now be elongated so that your back and legs are stretched out in a straight line.

6 Roll the shoulder blades back and down, creating a straight spine. Feel the muscles of the back move away from the spine, creating space. If possible, move the chest any amount closer to your thighs. Allow your head to drop downward and hang freely.

7 Hold the pose for three counts, directing the breath deep into the abdomen (each count is one full inhalation and exhalation). Release the pose by shifting the weight back onto your arms and shoulders. Lower yourself onto your hands and knees.

8 Repeat this pose three times. As you become familiar and strong in holding Down Dog Stretch, work up to holding the position for one to three minutes per repetition.

Headaches

The following techniques are highly effective in treating migraine or tension-type headaches:
a) Autogenic Training   b) Shoulder Rolls   c) Hoku Point

Autogenic Training

Origin: Johannes Schultz, a German psychiatrist and neurologist, developed autogenic training.

Objective: To lessen the pain and duration of migraine headaches

Frequency of use: Use as needed or three to four times per week. If you are experiencing a migraine, repeat this technique several times a day.

Duration: Sustain the technique for 15–20 minutes

Cross-reference: Use Abdominal Breathing (page 29) and Open Palms (page 24)

Difficulty level 1: Easy-to-follow steps

Complementary treatment: Progressive Muscle Relaxation (page 46)

This technique was developed in the 1930s. It has proven especially effective for treating migraine headaches.

1 Do this meditation in a lying-down or reclining position. Close your eyes...Engage in Abdominal Breathing...Breathe deeply, filling your body with fresh oxygen.

2 Concentrate on the qualities heavy and warm. Begin the first sequence by focusing on your right leg...Slowly repeat silently or out loud, "My right leg is heavy and warm, my right leg is heavy and warm, my right leg is heavy and warm, I am at peace" (or if you prefer, "I am completely calm").

3 Move to your left leg, repeating the phrase, "My left leg is heavy and warm," three times, followed by the phrase, "I am at peace," once. And then repeat, "Both of my legs are heavy and warm," three times, followed by, "I am at peace."

4 Progress to your right arm, repeating, "My right arm is heavy and warm," three times, followed by the phrase, "I am at peace," once.

5 Turn to your left arm and continue this sequence.

6 Focus on your heartbeat as you repeat, "My heartbeat is regular and calm, my heartbeat is regular and calm, my heartbeat is regular and calm, I am at peace."

7 Turn your attention to your breathing by repeating, "My breathing is calm and relaxed, my breathing is calm and relaxed, my breathing is calm and relaxed, I am at peace."

8 Focus on your abdomen. Repeat, "My abdomen is calm and relaxed, my abdomen is calm and relaxed, my abdomen is calm and relaxed, I am at peace."

9 Finally, focus on your forehead, repeating, "My forehead is cool, my forehead is cool, my forehead is cool, I am at peace."

10 At this point you have completed one sequence. Repeat the sequence for 15-20 minutes until the desired results are obtained. Complete the Autogenic Training by repeating, "Arms firm, breathe deeply, open my eyes."

Shoulder Rolls

Origin: Western medicine therapeutic exercise that frees blockages in the head, neck, and back, thereby releasing tension.

(🏃) **Objective: To alleviate simple or tension-type headache pain**

(🔄) **Frequency of use: May be used when needed**

(🕐) **Duration: Practice shoulder rolls for five minutes and repeat as needed**

(↔) **Cross-reference: Use Observing the Breath (page 28)**

(1) **Difficulty level 1: Try this technique first, but if you do not achieve the desired results, try Hoku Point (page 56)**

(🍃) **Complementary treatment: Progressive Muscle Relaxation (page 46)**

(+) **Quick remedy**

This simple technique can be used sitting in a chair at home or in the office. It is most effective when used repeatedly to teach the muscles of the neck and head to relax.

1 Sit comfortably in a chair with your feet planted firmly on the ground. Be relaxed but sit up straight, leaning forward slightly at your hips (this takes any strain off your lower back). Take a few deep inhalations, directing the breath all the way down to your lower belly.

2 Gently tip your head forward, being careful not to strain your muscles. Hold...Take one full breath. Gently tip your head backward. Hold... Take another full breath. Repeat this motion four to eight times.

3 Gently tilt your head to the right so that the right ear moves toward your right shoulder... Take a breath and hold for a count of three. Tilt your head to the left, moving your left ear toward your left shoulder. Take a breath and hold for a count of three. Repeat this motion four to eight times.

4 Raise both shoulders up as high as you can, reaching toward your ears...Tense them and hold for a count of "one one-thousand, two-one thousand, three one-thousand, four one-thousand"... Release abruptly with a "ha" sound. Repeat four times.

5 Roll your shoulders forward, creating openness across your upper back...Roll your shoulders up and backward. Repeat for 10 sets, focusing on your breath. Reverse the direction of your shoulder rolls by first rolling your shoulders back, then up and forward. Repeat for 10 sets.

Hoku Point

Origin: Age-old Eastern medicine practices. The Hoku point is a widely used acupressure point to relieve pain.

Objective: To alleviate headache pain caused by tension or stress

Frequency of use: May be used daily

Duration: Sustain meditation for 1–5 minutes

Cross-reference: Use Abdominal Breathing (page 29)

Difficulty level 1: This technique is easily performed

Complementary treatments: Breath Counting (page 57) and Pain Release (page 59)

Quick remedy

The Hoku point is an acupressure point widely used to relieve pain. It is located in the web of the finger, between your thumb and index finger (see photo). It is used to relieve general pain, especially headaches, arthritic pain, neck pain, shoulder pain, and toothache.

Caution: *Do not use this point if you are pregnant as it is believed to cause premature contractions.*

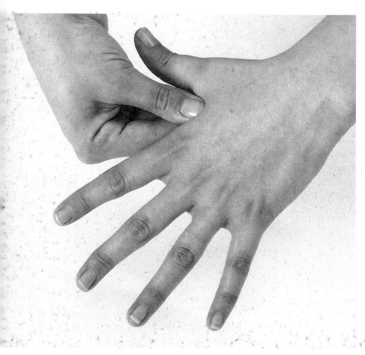

1 You may apply this treatment in any position that you find comfortable…Take a few deep-cleansing breaths.

2 Find the sorest spot on the muscle between your thumb and index finger on either hand. Press this point firmly with the thumb and index finger of your other hand. Press firmly enough to produce a mild pain…Hold and breathe.

3 Continue to hold as you gently move your head forward and backward as if you were indicating "yes." Breathe smoothly and regularly while holding this point for a minute or two, then switch to the other hand. Follow the same steps.

4 If the headache does not lessen, repeat the above steps or add the following movement. Hold the Hoku point and gently move your head from left to right as if indicating "no."…Then add the movement of dropping your right ear to your right shoulder then your left ear to your left shoulder. Make sure to hold this point for an equal time on both hands.

5 If you wish to try this point to alleviate pain in other parts of the body, try the following. For arthritis, hold the point while moving the joint that is in pain. If your knee is in pain, for example, hold the point while gently mobilizing the knee. For shoulder pain, hold the point while gently rolling the shoulder.

Chronic Pain

The following meditations are highly effective in managing chronic pain:

a) Breath Counting　　　　　b) Color Release　　　　　c) Pain Release

Breath Counting

⚕ **Objective: For severe pain and pain flare-ups**

⟳ **Frequency of use: May be used when needed**

◷ **Duration: 1–5 minutes**

↔ **Cross-reference: Use Open Palms (page 24)**

① **Difficulty level 1: Try this technique first to treat severe or sharp pain flare-ups**

🍃 **Complementary treatments: Pain Release (page 59) and Color Release (page 58)**

➕ **Quick remedy**

1 This sequence may be done standing or sitting.

2 Hold the inhalation for a count of four: "one one-thousand, two one-thousand, three one-thousand, four one thousand."

3 On the exhalation, count down from six: "six one-thousand, five one-thousand," etc...

4 Repeat for eight cycles or more.

A variation is to "quick sip" your breath. This requires taking quick, short inhalations through the nose. Do not use this technique if you have high blood pressure.

1 Take short, quick in-breaths to single beats... "one, two, three, four."

2 Exhale in long, slow breaths..."one one-thousand, two one-thousand, three one-thousand, four one-thousand." Repeat for eight cycles or more.

Color Release

Origin: Western; derived from the Focusing Method created by psychologist and philosopher Dr. Eugene Gendlin, University of Chicago.

Objective: **For chronic pain and pain flare-ups**

Frequency of use: **May be used when needed**

Duration: **Sustain technique for 5–10 minutes**

Cross-reference: **Use Abdominal Breathing (page 29) and Open Palms (page 24)**

Difficulty level 1: **Try this technique first to treat chronic and sharp pain**

Complementary treatment: **Pain Release (page 59)**

Quick remedy

1 Choose your preferred sitting or lying-down position and take a few moments to get comfortable...Close your eyes and engage in Abdominal Breathing.

2 When you feel sufficiently relaxed, turn your attention to the place in your body where you are experiencing pain. Make a few inquiries into the pain...Where do you feel the pain the strongest? How intense is the pain? What qualities does it have?

3 If your pain had a color, what color would it be?

4 Focus on that color...Breathe deeply.

5 What color would dissolve the pain?

6 Inhale and bring in that dissolving color... Feel it slowly dissolving the pain...As you exhale, release the original color of the pain and replace it with the dissolving pain.

7 Repeat for several cycles until you feel you have released some of the pain in that area.

8 Turn your attention to any other areas of your body that are in pain. Complete this exercise by taking a few natural inhalations and exhalations and open your eyes.

Pain Release

Origin: Eastern; derived from Zen Buddhist mindfulness meditation.

(人) **Objective: To treat chronic pain**

(↻) **Frequency of use: May be used as often as needed**

(⏱) **Duration: 10–15 minutes**

(↔) **Cross-reference: Use Abdominal Breathing (page 29) and Open Palms (page 24)**

(1) **Difficulty level 2: Requires ability to sustain focus**

(✿) **Complementary treatment: Passive Relaxation (page 48)**

Note: *If you begin to feel discomfort or your pain levels become too intense, simply open your eyes, end the visualization, and try again at a later time.*

1 Choose a comfortable sitting or reclining position that allows your body to be relaxed and fully supported. Close your eyes and engage in Abdominal Breathing...Allow space for any uncomfortable or painful sensations in your body to simply be present at this time.

2 Direct your attention to a location within your body where you have been experiencing pain or discomfort...Allow the breath to move you gently toward these sensations.

3 Observe any emotions or thoughts you have in relation to the pain...Breathe and give yourself the suggestion that it is safe to explore this pain and to feel whatever sensations arise.

4 Begin an inquiry...How can I describe the pain?...Is it specific and bundled like a hard knot or is the discomfort more generalized?...Does it have a texture?...Is it heavy or light?...Is the pain dull, throbbing, tingling, or burning?

5 Gently direct your breath to the tissues surrounding the pain...The breath carries a peaceful light that infuses the tissues with warmth... creating space for the pain simply to be there.

6 Breathe into the pain...The breath allows you to enter the pain, making room for the discomfort. As you accept the pain, you can then release it.

7 The pain softens into the wholeness of your body...The breath creates the space to feel... to accept...to let go...and to heal.

8 The breath loosens any tightness or tension around the tissues, tendons, muscles, or bones surrounding the pain...The weight of the pain detaches from this area and begins to float away...Feel a lightness as the weight of the pain lifts and carries you to rest in a safe vessel on water.

9 Rest comfortably in this vessel, floating weightlessly...The breath gently rocks you on the water...Experience the peaceful feeling of timelessness...Let go into the peace and freedom of release...

10 You may stay in this place as long as you need...As your energy is replenished imagine a beautiful gold sun floating above your head...Allow its warmth and light to flow down into your body...Return your attention to your entire body...Begin to feel weight and heaviness within your body...Wiggle your fingers and toes.

11 Count down slowly from 10 to 1...Open your eyes.

Fatigue and Lethargy

The following techniques alleviate fatigue and lethargy:

a) Reiki Self-healing: Recycling the Vital Force

b) Mental Sponge: Recalling Your Vital Life Force   c) Kidney Charge/Color Charge

Reiki Self-healing: Recycling the Vital Force

Origin: Reiki is a Japanese art of healing thought to be thousands of years old and to have originated as a Tibetan Buddhist practice.

🏃 **Objective: To treat fatigue and lethargy**

🕖 **Frequency of use: May be used daily or several times a day**

🕐 **Duration: Sustain for 1–5 minutes**

↔ **Cross-reference: Use Open Palms (page 24) and Observing the Breath (page 28)**

① **Difficulty level 1: Easy to administer**

🌿 **Complementary treatment: Gold Ball Scan (page 45)**

➕ **Quick remedy**

The Japanese healing art of reiki (pronounced ray-key) is a system of laying on hands to improve health and balance the mind, body, and spirit. When first practicing Reiki Self-healing, it is best to do so daily for the first month.

1 Choose a comfortable sitting position. Close your eyes. Take a few deep breaths...On the next inhalation, raise your shoulders toward your ears and exhale, dropping the shoulders abruptly and making a "ha" sound. Repeat several times.

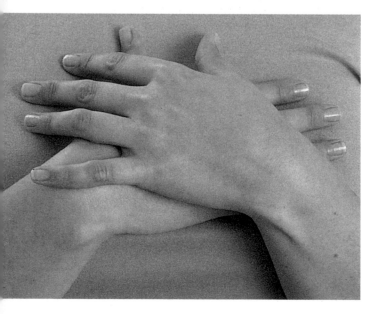

2 Bring your hands up to your heart center at the sternum with your palms facing downward. Place your left hand over your right hand; breathe deeply...Turn inward as you anchor your mind to the breath...Draw your life force back from the expenditures of the day.

3 Your life force returns in waves of energy... The energy enters through your hands and into the heart center...It then begins to be recycled into your body.

4 Visualize a beautiful, golden energy from the universe connecting to the back of your hands...Lift your hands and place them just below your collarbones...The palms face downward and the hands rest end to end with fingers pointing toward one another.

5 This compassionate universal life force channels through your hands into your body. As it enters your body, it mixes with your own life force, returning your body to balance and harmony.

6 Breathe naturally while holding this hand position for up to five minutes. When you are ready to finish, drop your hands to your lap...In your own manner, give thanks for the energy you received. Open your eyes and return your attention to your external surroundings.

Mental Sponge: Recalling Your Vital Life Force

Origin: Derived from mystical teachings of Rosicrucian tradition.

(人) **Objective: For moderate and/or ongoing fatigue**

(⏱) **Frequency of use: May be used daily**

(◉) **Duration: 10–15 minutes**

(↔) **Cross-reference: Use Cupped Hands (page 25) and Abdominal Breathing (page 29)**

(①) **Difficulty level 2: Technique requires ability to sustain concentration**

(✎) **Complementary treatment: The Observer (page 32)**

The "mental sponge" is a powerful tool that can help you to reclaim and revitalize your precious life force. You teach yourself to reclaim your life force from memories, places, people, events, and thoughts.

1 Choose your preferred seated position. Close your eyes and engage in Abdominal Breathing... Let any tension from the day's activities wash away as you are led to a place in your mind that is calm and untouched by the activities and thoughts of the day.

2 Begin the process of collecting back your vital life force. In your mind's eye, create the image of a sponge. This sponge can be any material, shape, or size. You may want to use a small sponge that has a large capacity to expand. This sponge is a bright white or gold color.

3 Send the sponge around your home into the main living room...Notice where you have left energy behind...Watch as the sponge soaks up your life force...Remain relaxed and connected to your breath...Allow the sponge to do the work.

4 Send the sponge to the kitchen and dining area to collect energy that may have been left there...The sponge grows bright with your life force...

5 Send the sponge to the bathroom...Perhaps you left energy behind when you were rushing off to work or an appointment.

6 If the sponge begins to feel as if it is overflowing, bring it back to your body and squeeze it out...Send the sponge to your bedroom... Perhaps you left energy in your sleep and dream time...

7 Send your sponge to your workplace...Notice energy you may have left behind in a project, problem, or conversation with a coworker...Send it to your daily calendar...Notice any energy you may already have invested in future events...Let your sponge call this future energy back to the present.

8 Call the sponge back to your body, placing it one foot (30 cm) above your head...Form a giant gold sun around it...This sun infuses your returning life force with universal chi...With each breath, the gold sun gets brighter and warmer...

9 Wring the sponge out, letting the energy descend into your body...Soak up this energy, directing it first to the lower belly and lower back region... Direct the chi to the area of your solar plexus and chest...Direct the chi to your upper body and head.

10 Return to waking consciousness by counting backward from 10 to 1...Open your eyes and give your body a long, leisurely stretch.

You may also send the sponge to call energy back from a relationship, a problem, or a future project.

Kidney Charge/Color Charge

Kidney Charge

Origin: Breema bodywork therapy originating from the Kurdish village of Breemava in the mountains between Iran and Afghanistan. According to Eastern medical philosophy, the kidneys and adrenal glands are the storehouse for your body's energy reserves. The Kidney Charge and Color Charge send an energetic impulse to the kidneys and adrenal glands, promoting balance and harmony and combating fatigue.

- ⊛ **Objective: To alleviate fatigue**
- ⟳ **Frequency of use: May be used daily**
- ⓣ **Duration: 1–5 minutes**
- ↔ **Cross-reference: Abdominal Breathing (page 29)**

- ① **Difficulty level 1: Requires a small degree of flexibility**
- ⊘ **Complementary treatment: Chakra Cleansing and Balancing (page 34)**
- ⊕ **Quick remedy**

1 Sit in a simple cross-legged position or with the soles together, knees relaxed and open to the side.

2 Take a breath in and lean forward...Gently stretch your arms out in front of you. Take another breath in...Reach any amount further forward, allowing the lower back to open gently.

3 Take a breath in and straighten your spine. Lean forward again while taking your arms behind your back. Vigorously slap the kidneys, just above the waist, with alternating open palms and fingers closed. Slap the kidneys for three full breaths.

4 Inhale and straighten your back. Lean forward again, vigorously slapping the kidneys with alternating palms for three breaths. Repeat four to eight times.

5 Sit comfortably and quietly for a moment or two.

2

3

Color Charge

1 Begin in your preferred sitting position. Close your eyes and engage in Abdominal Breathing.

2 When you feel sufficiently relaxed, focus your attention on your third center at the solar plexus (associated with regulating kidney function).

3 Visualize a vibrant yellow energy ball spinning clockwise in your solar plexus. Focus and breathe into this yellow color for one to five minutes.

4 When you are ready, release the color and open your eyes. Do this color visualization at the solar plexus daily for 21 days.

Insomnia

Tips for a Good Night's Sleep

- Go to bed and get up at the same time each day.
- Limit or avoid naps as they can interfere with nighttime sleeping.
- Avoid caffeine, nicotine, and alcohol late in the evening.
- Take regular exercise.
- Limit your fluid intake close to bedtime to reduce nighttime toilet visits.
- Establish a routine to help you relax before bed, such as taking a bath, reading, or listening to music.
- Avoid using your bed for anything other than sleep.
- Make a to-do list before you go to bed to help relieve worries that keep you awake at night.
- If you can't fall asleep, don't fight it. Get up and distract yourself by reading or doing some other nonstimulating activity.

The following meditations can help relieve insomnia:

a) Calming Breath   b) Yoga Mudra

Calming Breath

Origin: Combination of Eastern Zen Buddhism and Western self-hypnosis approaches to calm the mind and body through breath focusing.

🚶 **Objective: To help you sleep**

🔄 **Frequency of use: May be used nightly**

🕐 **Duration: 5–10 minutes**

↔ **Cross-reference: Use with Yoga Mudra (page 66)**

① **Difficulty level 1: Easily executed**

🌿 **Complementary treatment: Progressive Muscle Relaxation (page 46)**

➕ **Quick remedy**

1 Lie comfortably on your back or side. Focus on Abdominal Breathing...Relax your body.

2 Count backward slowly from ten to one while visualizing your body becoming heavier and heavier with each count..."Ten one-thousand...Nine one-thousand"...Gently let go..."Eight one-thousand... Seven one-thousand...Six one-thousand...Five one-thousand"...Let go more deeply..."Four one-thousand...Three one-thousand"...Let go and relax..."Two one-thousand...one one-thousand."

3 Start to count down from ten once again. Give yourself over to the weight and heaviness of your body...Feel yourself sinking deeper and deeper...

4 Return to the top of the count and count down again, giving yourself the suggestion of slipping deeper and deeper into relaxation.

5 If your mind wanders, simply return it to the breath. Repeat these cycles of counting until you slip naturally into sleep.

Yoga Mudra

Origin: Roots in Hatha and Tantric yoga. The Sanskrit translation for yoga mudra is "The Yogic Gesture," and it is known, among many other benefits, to aid in calming the mind.

(🏃) **Objective: To help you sleep**

(🕐) **Frequency of use: May be used on a regular basis**

(🕐) **Duration: 5–10 minutes**

(↔) **Cross-reference: Use with Calming Breath (page 64)**

(①) **Difficulty level 1: Simple pose that requires a small degree of flexibility**

(🍃) **Complementary treatment: Autogenic Training (page 54)**

(⊕) **Quick remedy**

1 For this pose you will need several pillows (unless you have a high degree of flexibility). Stack them in front of you so that they reach your waist or chest level when you are sitting. They should be close enough for you to reach them easily when you bend forward. Sit in front of the pillows on the floor in an open, cross-legged position. Place one foot against the other so that your ankles line up.

2 Place your hands behind your back with your palms facing outward. With your right hand, gently hold your left wrist.

3 Inhale deeply. As you exhale, slowly begin to bend forward over your knees to place your forehead on the pillows. This is a symbolic gesture of surrendering the activity of the mind to the calmness of the heart (if you feel an uncomfortable stretch in your hips, place more pillows in your stack). Release your thoughts or concerns into the pillows.

4 Take a breath in and exhale as you bring your body upright again.

5 Repeat the sequence and add a count to your breath...Inhale and exhale, bending forward, while counting to eight...Try to use the full count of eight in placing your forehead on the pillows. Hold for a count of four...Inhale to a count of eight as you return your body upright. Hold for a count of four and exhale. Take a breath and repeat the sequence.

6 Go at your own pace, repeating this sequence for eight cycles.

Immune Deficiency

The following techniques help strengthen the immune system:

a) Thymus Tap   b) Activating the Immune Response

Thymus Tap

Origin: Energy medicine of Eastern origin. Tapping the thymus for five minutes daily is believed to stimulate the immune response.

(🏃) **Objective: To strengthen the immune system**

(⏱) **Frequency of use: Use each morning**

(⏰) **Duration: 5 minutes**

(↔) **Cross-reference: Use Abdominal Breathing (page 29)**

(1) **Difficulty level 1: A straightforward technique to use daily**

(🍃) **Complementary treatment: Activating the Immune Response (page 68)**

(+) **Quick remedy**

Tap the thymus when you are ill or feeling particularly stressed, or use as a preventive technique for five minutes every morning.

1 Locate the thymus gland in the upper chest (see photo).

2 With your first three fingers, begin tapping this area. Tap vigorously to activate the gland.

3 Sustain tapping for five full minutes while focusing on Abdominal Breathing.

4 Repeat several times a day if you are fighting an illness or feeling particularly stressed.

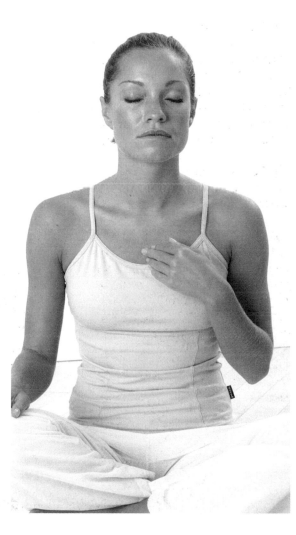

Activating the Immune Response

Origin: Western/Eastern mix combining Western medical knowledge with Eastern energy practices to increase immune response ability.

⚕ **Objective: To strengthen the immune system**

⟳ **Frequency of use: Up to once daily**

⏱ **Duration: 15–20 minutes**

↔ **Cross-reference: Use Open Palms (page 24) and Grounding Cord (page 41)**

① **Difficulty level 2: Technique requires ability to sustain concentration**

🍃 **Complementary treatment: Lymph Drainage (page 76)**

1 Choose a comfortable sitting or reclining position. Close your eyes softly, gently inhale and exhale through your nose, releasing any tension.

2 Use your full inhalation and exhalation, allowing for a slight pause between each breath... The breath carries healing energy to replenish your body...Oxygen flows into every cell...On the exhalation toxins are gently lifted and washed away. The energy of these toxins flushes down your grounding cord and into the earth.

3 Focus on the long bones of your arms and legs. The breath enters the soft tissue in the hollow shafts of these bones. Here in the bone marrow immune system cells are manufactured.

4 See these white immune "helper cells," used to fight infection...See them being energized with a bright blue light...Silently say, "My immune cells are healthy and vital."

5 These energized cells move out into the body to the nodes. These bean-shaped lymph nodes are concentrated in clusters in the side of the neck, breasts, armpits, abdomen, and groin (see illustration). The blue light of the helper cells enters the nodes and radiates throughout the neck, breasts, armpits, abdomen, and groin.

6 The light branches out into the lymphatic vessels, a complex highway of vessels...Your body intuitively guides your awareness along this highway of blue light...The light is carried into your organs and distributed throughout the body.

7 The helper cells patrol the body, searching for free radicals, toxins, and impurities. The blue light gently lifts waste materials to be cleansed and eliminated...Take a few deep-cleansing breaths, drawing in fresh oxygen to help the healing process...

8 Redirect your attention to the simple inhalation and exhalation of the breath.

9 Allow your body to remain in a state of calm and rest as you return your awareness to your entire body. When you are ready, open your eyes and give yourself a good long stretch.

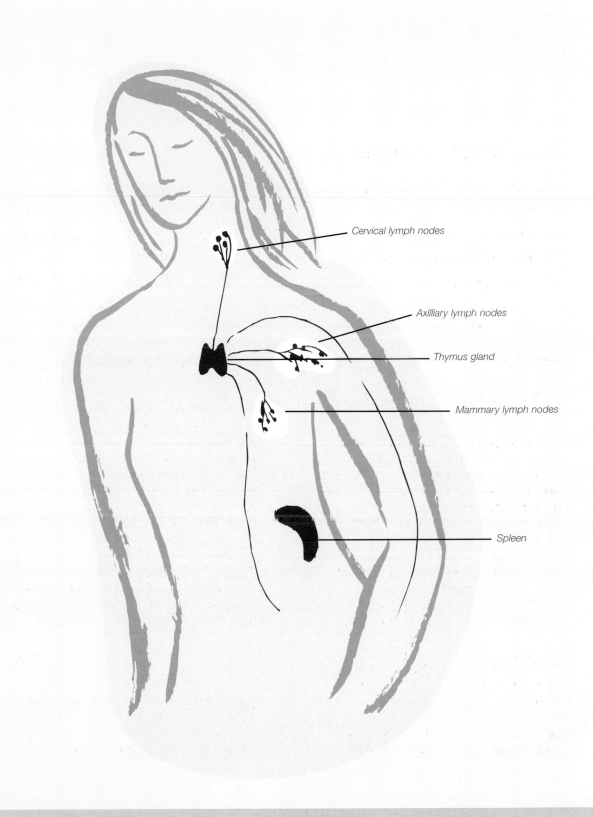

Cervical lymph nodes

Axilliary lymph nodes

Thymus gland

Mammary lymph nodes

Spleen

These parts of the body play an important role in helping to develop a strong immune system.

Nausea

The following treatments help reduce nausea:

a) Reflexology Point   b) Gentle Twist

Reflexology Point

Origin: Reflexology is a pressure-point therapy believed to date back to ancient Egypt and has roots in the Chinese and Japanese cultures.

- 🚶 **Objective: To treat mild to moderate nausea**

- ⏱ **Frequency of use: Use as needed**

- ⏰ **Duration: 2–5 minutes on each foot**

- ↔ **Cross-reference: Use Counting the Breath (page 27) and Grounding (page 30)**

- ① **Difficulty level 1: Technique is easily administered**

- 🍃 **Complementary treatment: Autogenic Training (page 54)**

- ➕ **Quick remedy**

Reflexology is an ancient therapy involving pressure points on the feet. It is believed that the bottom of the foot contains reflex points that correspond to the various organs and nerves within the body.

Place this book nearby so you can refer to the photo. The nausea point is not traditionally marked on the main reflexology chart; it is located down in the lung and bronchial area, directly below the third toe.

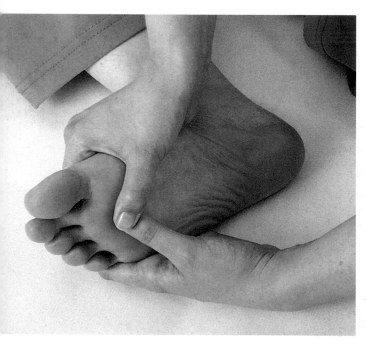

1 Choose a comfortable sitting position and remove your shoes and socks. If it is comfortable, sit with the soles together, allowing your knees to fall out to the sides.

2 Locate the nausea point, down in the lung and bronchial area, directly below the third toe (see photo). Place your thumbs in this area on each foot in turn.

3 Breathe in deeply and press firmly on this point... You may notice a soreness or tenderness in this area. On your next inhalation, breathe in to a count of four and slowly exhale to a count of eight while applying constant pressure. Repeat this for three cycles.

4 Now press in and up at the same time, moving the thumb pressure toward the toes in a continual stroking motion...Continue this motion as you breathe in to a count of four and slowly exhale to a count of eight. Repeat for a cycle of eight.

5 Place both feet back on the floor to help ground out any toxins your body is releasing. Take a few cleansing breaths to complete the exercise. Repeat as necessary.

Gentle Twist

Origin: Hatha yoga posture that twists the body at the solar plexus center, believed to thereby relieve nausea.

🏃 **Objective: To reduce mild to moderate nausea**

🔄 **Frequency of use: Use as needed**

⏱ **Duration: 1–5 minutes**

↔ **Cross-reference: Use Counting the Breath (page 27)**

① **Difficulty level 1: Technique is easily executed**

✍ **Complementary treatments: Autogenic Training (page 54) or Counting the Breath (page 27)**

➕ **Quick remedy**

1 Do this exercise lying down, either on the floor or preferably on a bed. Lie on your back with your knees bent and feet flat on the floor. Stretch your arms out to each side at shoulder level, forming a "T."

2 Inhale, and as you exhale, allow your knees to drop gently over to the right...Breathe slowly and calmly for three full breaths...Bring your knees upright and center your hips...Now allow your knees to drop gently to the left while taking three full breaths.

3 Bring your knees upright and center your hips. Now add a count to the breath. Inhale through your nose to a count of four, and exhale slowly from your

mouth to a count of eight. Try to emotionally detach from the nausea by "watching" the sensations that rise and fall away. When you feel ready, bring your knees upright and center your hips.

4 Drop your knees to the left. Inhale through your nose to a count of four and exhale slowly from your mouth to a count of eight. Repeat this pattern of breath as, again, you focus on observing the nausea.

5 When you feel ready, return your knees upright and center your hips. Roll over to your right side. Lie here for a few moments and breathe regularly. Push yourself up with both hands to a seated position. Take a minute to readjust.

Low-grade Fever

The following treatments can be effective in reducing fever:

a) Drawing Out the Heat   b) Cooling Breath   c) Cool Blue Chakras

Drawing Out the Heat

Origin: Based on Western guided imagery.

🏃 **Objective: To reduce fever**

🕐 **Frequency of use: Use as needed**

⏱ **Duration: 10–15-minute segments, repeated as required**

↔ **Cross-reference: Use Grounding (page 30)**

① **Difficulty level 1: Try this technique first to treat fever**

🌿 **Complementary treatment: Cooling Breath (page 73)**

⊕ **Quick remedy**

This technique is designed to draw the heat out of your body through the feet. You will need a thick pair of socks, preferably made of wool.

1 As well as the woolen socks, you will need cold water, a towel, and a warm blanket. Soak the socks in cold water or ice.

2 Sit in a straight-backed chair. Put on the wet socks and place your feet on the towel so that the soles are firmly planted on the floor. Wrap the blanket around your body.

3 Close your eyes and begin to focus on your breath for a few cycles...On your next out-breath, picture a light being exhaled through the soles...This light forms roots that reach into the earth. With each breath, the roots reach further and further into the earth until you feel a strong, secure connection. These roots will help to draw the fever out of your body.

4 Imagine the fever as a red heat that fills your body from head to toe. Feel the gravitational force drawing this heat downward, draining it from your head, neck, and shoulders...The heat moves downward through your upper back, midsection, and lower back...Continue to breathe slowly and calmly as the heat flows down your legs into your feet and out of the soles into the earth.

5 The coolness of the socks helps to draw the heat out of your body as you send it down through the roots into the earth. Continue to ground out the heat until you achieve the desired results. If necessary, soak the socks again and repeat the exercise. When you are ready, remove the socks and replace them with dry ones.

Cooling Breath

Origin: Western breathwork technique.

🚶 **Objective: To reduce fever**

🕔 **Frequency of use: Use as needed to lower fever**

🕐 **Duration: 1–3 minutes, repeating as necessary**

↔ **Cross-reference: Use Abdominal Breathing (page 29)**

① **Difficulty level 1: Simple to carry out**

🌿 **Complementary treatment: Drawing Out the Heat (page 72)**

➕ **Quick remedy**

This simple breathing technique helps reduce fever. You breathe with your mouth slightly open to cool your body It is similar in principle to a dog panting to relieve heat.

1 You can do this technique in any position. Open your mouth slightly, letting your tongue rest gently behind the lower teeth. On the inhalation, draw the breath across your tongue, feeling the moisture on your tongue. Slowly inhale to a count of four.

2 On the exhalation, keep the mouth slightly open as you send the breath back across the tongue, while slowly counting to four.

3 On the next inhalation, imagine drawing in an icy blue mist as you feel the moisture moving over your tongue, cooling your body. On the exhalation, imagine the heat being exhaled as a warm mist across your tongue.

4 Repeat this breathing pattern for 1–3 minutes. Return to your normal breathing and, if necessary, repeat the open-mouthed breathing.

Cool Blue Chakras

Origin: Western breathwork technique.

◉ **Objective: To cool a fever**

◉ **Frequency of use: Use as needed**

◉ **Duration: 5–10 minutes**

◉ **Cross-reference: Use Abdominal Breathing (page 29) and Grounding Cord (page 41)**

① **Difficulty level 2: Highly effective technique to treat a persistent fever**

◉ **Complementary treatment: Cooling Breath (page 73)**

While this is a highly effective technique, it can take longer to reduce the fever than the previous techniques.

1 Choose a comfortable, straight-backed chair. Close your eyes and anchor your mind to your breath.

2 Create a grounding cord and give the weight of your body over to the chair.

3 Turn your attention to the crown chakra, the energy center on the top of your head. See a clear blue block of ice forming at this center.

4 Breathe in and draw the blue ice down into the sixth chakra at the center of the head. Feel the ice cooling your head, the blood vessels constricting slowly to decrease the fever.

5 The ice melts downward into your throat, spreading soothing, cool relief with each breath...

6 The blue ice slides down to the heart chakra... The cool ice spreads throughout the chest and upper back, slowly cooling and dropping the temperature of the fever.

7 Breathe naturally as the icy blue mist penetrates the third chakra at the solar plexus...The coolness of the blue relaxes and calms the body.

8 The cool ice continues to melt downward to fill the second chakra, about two to three finger widths below your navel...This center begins to fill with a misty blue...

9 The breath continues to draw this cool blue downward to the first chakra, located at the tailbone...The blue dissolves and cools the red of this center...Imagine your temperature dropping another degree.

10 Once you have reached this lowest chakra, return your attention to the top of your head and see the blue icy mist flowing like a cool river along your spine...Take eight complete breaths using this image. When you are ready, open your eyes and drink a glass of cool water.

Cold/Flu/Sore Throat

The following techniques are effective at treating colds, flu, and sore throat:
a) Cleansing the Lymph Glands   b) Lymph Drainage

Cleansing the Lymph Glands

Origin: Bruce Chikly, a medical doctor from France, developed Lymph Drainage Therapy. This therapeutic technique involves subtle manual maneuvers to aid in the recirculation of lymph, which speeds the removal of impurities and toxins.

Objective: To cleanse the lymph glands

Frequency of use: Use as needed

Duration: Sustain for 15–20 minutes

Cross-reference: Use Grounding Cord (page 41)

Difficulty level 1: A quick way to cleanse toxins from the body

Complementary treatment: Lymph Drainage (page 76)

Quick remedy

This treatment should be done in the bath; to help you relax, use a bath pillow to support your neck.

Choose one of the following treatments:
- 1–2 handfuls of mineral salts and 1–2 cups of apple cider vinegar (these ingredients will draw toxins out of the lymph glands)
- 1/4 cup of milk or cream, 3 drops of chamomile oil, 3 drops of lavender oil, and 3 drops of rosemary oil (this will alleviate tension and relax the blood vessels)

Caution: *The above essential oils should be treated with care. Although they are considered benign herbs for external treatment, they must not be ingested. Always test your skin for an allergic reaction— dilute the above ingredients in water and apply to a small patch of skin on your arm. If any redness appears within 24 hours, do not use this ingredient.*

1 Prepare a warm to hot bath, adding your choice of the above treatments.

2 Settle into the bathwater and allow your neck and head to rest on the back of the tub. Take a few deep-cleansing breaths as you allow the warmth of the water to penetrate deeply into your muscles.

3 Create a grounding cord to energetically release toxins and any energy blocks.

4 Visualize your lymph glands. The major glands are clustered behind the ears, along the sides of the neck, under the armpits, and in the abdominal cavity and groin. These glands move and cleanse the fluids in your body. The lymph glands connect into a vast network of lymphatic vessels, much like our circulatory system.

5 Move your hands back and forth on the surface of the water, imitating the rhythm of the ocean as the waves slowly lap the sand...The rhythm of the water pulsates through your body, moving through the lymph vessels...See the major lymph nodes being cleansed with the movement of the water...The pulsating rhythm gently lifts and carries away toxins...

6 Focus on your grounding cord...The energy of the toxins gathers at the base of your spine and is released down your grounding cord into the earth...As it reaches the earth it is neutralized and recycled into fresh energy...Breathe deeply, directing the toxins to flush from your body and down the cord...

7 Return your focus to the simple flow of the inhalation and exhalation.

8 To complete this cleansing meditation, rinse yourself with fresh water so that any remaining toxic residue is washed down the drain.

Lymph Drainage

(人) **Objective: To improve lymph circulation**

(↻) **Frequency of use: Use daily or as needed**

(⏱) **Duration: Do in 5-minute segments**

(↔) **Cross-reference: Use Abdominal Breathing (page 29)**

(1) **Difficulty level 1: Simple to administer**

(🍃) **Complementary treatment: Activating the Immune Response (page 68)**

(➕) **Quick remedy**

This therapeutic technique involves subtle manual maneuvers to help the recirculation of lymph, which speeds the removal of impurities and toxins.

1 The diagram on page 77 illustrates the lymph system in the neck and clavicle (collarbone) region.

2 Start by opening the main thoracic duct located just below the collarbone. Bring your fingers together and place the back of your fingers on the sides of your neck (see photo).

3 Very lightly begin to move your fingers downward in a stroking motion. Move toward the hollows behind the collarbones, aiming slightly in the direction of the heart...The stroking motion begins about midway down the neck. Press in and down for a count of three and release for three... Move your fingers down the neck and then return to midway...Use lightweight, superficial movements, as if you are stroking the skin. Repeat three to five times.

4 Move your fingers up the neck in a progressive manner, starting at the base. The stroking

moves the lymph, which flows like the ocean. Press in and down for a count of three and release for three...Place your fingers slightly higher on your neck and repeat...Press in for three...Release for three...Continue this upward movement until you reach the area behind your ears at the top of your neck.

5 The area behind the ears is known as the Water Wheel. Press a bit harder here, but still keep the touch lightweight. Press in for three, moving the stroke downward...Release for three...Move your fingers slightly lower on the neck, pressing in for three...Release for three...Repeat this cycle for three sets.

6 Starting again at the base of the neck on the second cycle, place the back of your fingers toward the back of your neck...Press in for a count of three and release for three...Continue this motion up the back of the neck and then down the neck, returning the fluid to the thoracic duct located in the hollows behind the collarbone...

7 Reverse this movement to direct the lymph down the neck toward the thoracic duct... Repeat this cycle for a set of three.

Improving circulation of the lymph system in the neck area will help with the removal of toxins and impurities.

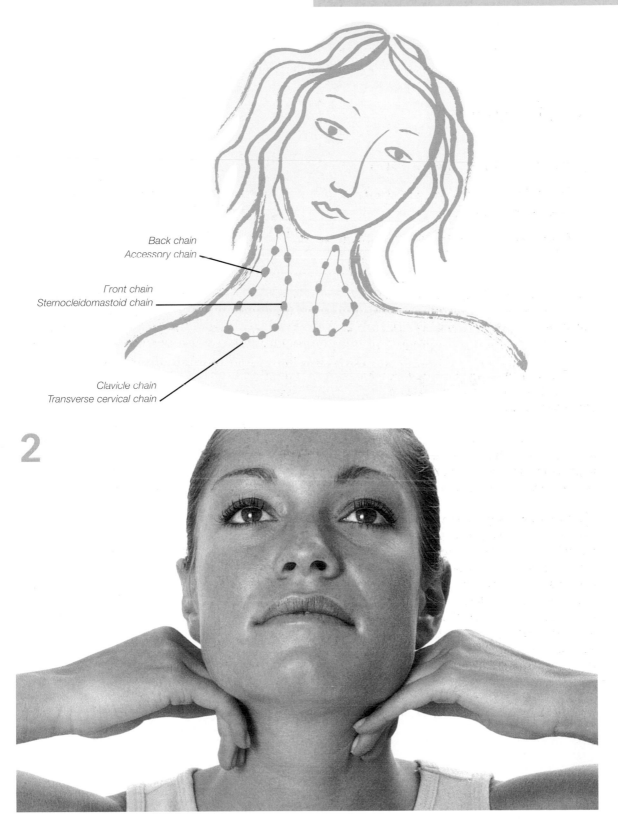

Back chain
Accessory chain

Front chain
Sternocleidomastoid chain

Clavicle chain
Transverse cervical chain

2

Sinus Congestion

Contact your health-care provider if:

- Redness or swelling occurs on the eyelids or cheeks (a sign of infection).
- Sinus congestion lasts more than a week.
- You have a fever for more than a week.
- Nasal secretions become yellow or green with sinus pressure.

The following techniques are effective in treating sinus congestion:

a) Sinus Tap   b) Forward Fold—Uttanasana   c) Clearing the Sinus Passages

Sinus Tap

Origin: Energy medicinal approach of Eastern origin.

⍝ **Objective: To relieve sinus congestion**

⟳ **Frequency of use: Use as needed**

◷ **Duration: Tap for 1–5 minutes and repeat as required**

↔ **Cross-reference: Use Observing the Breath (page 28)**

① **Difficulty level 1: Try this technique first to relieve congestion**

🍃 **Complementary treatments: Lymph Drainage (page 76) and Hoku Point (page 56)**

⊕ **Quick remedy**

1 This exercise can be done while standing or sitting. Place your fingers at the top of your cheekbones, an inch or so below the eyes.

2 Tap your fingers vigorously and quickly over the cheekbones. This stimulates the sinus cavity and helps to move fluids. This tapping may cause some discomfort, depending on how tender the sinus cavities feel...Concentrate on your breath.

3 Now alternate the tapping from right to left fingers, starting next to your nose and moving your fingers outward across your cheekbones.

4 Move your hands to above the eyebrow and repeat the vigorous tapping while focusing on your breath. Then switch to alternating the tapping from right to left fingers, starting at the midpoint just over and above the eyes. Tap your fingers outward toward your temples.

5 End with a few deep breaths.

3

Forward Fold—Uttanasana

Origin: Tantric, Hatha, and various yoga traditions. This forward posture increases blood flow to the head, helping to open sinus passages.

🚶 **Objective: To relieve sinus congestion**

🔄 **Frequency of use: Use as needed**

⏱ **Duration: 1–2 minutes, repeating as required**

↔ **Cross-reference: Use Abdominal Breathing (page 29)**

① **Difficulty level 1: Try this technique if you are able to bend forward without too much discomfort**

🌿 **Complementary treatment: Lymph Drainage (page 76)**

➕ **Quick remedy**

Caution: Do not use this technique if you have high blood pressure.

1 This pose is done standing. Stand with your back about 12 inches (30 cm) from a wall.

2 Bend your knees so as not to strain your lower back. Slowly begin to fold forward, gently allowing your hips and buttocks to be supported by the wall if necessary. Release any tension in your neck, allowing the head to relax completely and your shoulders and arms to dangle freely.

3 Drop your mouth open slightly as you concentrate on your breath. Your head continues to move toward the floor. Go forward only to a comfortable range, being careful not to strain the lower back or back of the legs.

4 Rest in this position, allowing the full weight of your upper body to move toward the floor. You may experience pressure in your head from the congested sinus passages. This is to be expected. This inverted position will enhance blood and fluid circulation to the head and through the passages. Focus intensely on your breath...The movement of the oxygen cleanses the cavities of the sinuses... The breath soothes the inflamed passages and gently begins to open them, allowing oxygen to flow more freely...

5 Hold the position for one to two minutes while focusing on the breath. Slowly roll to an upright position. Move slowly to minimize any feelings of dizziness or light-headedness.

2

Clearing the Sinus Passages

Origin: Western; guided imagery based on Western medicine.

Objective: To relieve chronic congestion

Frequency of use: Use as needed

Duration: 5–7 minutes, repeating as necessary

Cross-reference: Use Abdominal Breathing (page 29) and Grounding (page 30)

Difficulty level 2: Requires ability to sustain concentration

Complementary treatment: Lymph Drainage (page 76)

1 Choose your preferred sitting position. Close your eyes softly and start to engage in Abdominal Breathing.

2 Take a breath and plug your nose with your forefinger and thumb. With your mouth closed, gently blow as if you were blowing up a balloon. This forces air into the middle ear and quickly opens the Eustachian tubes. You may feel a mild to moderate pressure, depending on your level of congestion.

3 Refocus on your breath...Visualize your Eustachian tubes leading from your throat to the inside of the ear. The tubes are located at the back of the nose behind the soft palate, and lead up and back at an angle of about 45 degrees toward the inner ear.

4 Imagine that you can breathe inwardly through the tube as if you were drawing on a straw...See a bright blue-violet light...This light travels from the back of the nose at the soft palate along the path to the inner ear.

5 Focus on your breath as you concentrate on this blue-violet light radiating through the tubes and up into the sinus cavities. The cavities are located as pockets above and behind your eyes, behind your cheekbones, and behind your upper teeth. Imagine the colored light moving into these areas and dissolving the blockages in the tubes and sinuses.

6 The breath begins to move the energy blockage down the throat...See it releasing all the way down to your grounding cord and out into the earth.

7 Continue to focus both on releasing the blocked energy and on the radiating blue light.

8 When you are ready, return your attention to the simple inhalation and exhalation of the breath... Open your eyes.

Asthma/Bronchial Problems

The following meditations are helpful in addressing asthma and other bronchial problems:
a) Reflexology Lung Points   b) Bronchial Opening

Reflexology Lung Points

Origin: Reflexology is a pressure-point therapy believed to date back to ancient Egypt and has roots in the Chinese and Japanese cultures.

(🏃) **Objective: To relieve lung congestion and open bronchial passages**

(🌀) **Frequency of use: Use as needed**

(◎) **Duration: 10 minutes**

(↔) **Cross-reference: Use Abdominal Breathing (page 29) and Grounding (page 30)**

(1) **Difficulty level 1: Easily administered technique**

(🌿) **Complementary treatment: Bronchial Opening (page 83)**

(➕) **Quick remedy**

1 Sit barefoot in a comfortable position. Begin with either foot. Cross your foot over your thigh so that the sole is facing upward. Take the foot in your hand and place your thumbs on the lung point (see illustration). As you can see, the lung point spans across the upper part of the ball of the foot.

2 Place both thumbs next to each other and press firmly into this point. You may notice a soreness or tenderness in this area. Breathe in deeply to a count of four and slowly exhale to a count of eight, while applying constant pressure. Repeat for eight cycles.

3 Now begin to alternate your thumbs, applying pressure first through one thumb, then the other. Massage the area with a back-and-forth motion, slowly trying to go a bit deeper with each push of the thumb. Continue to focus on counting your breath.

4 Switch to your other foot. Repeat for up to five minutes each side.

5 When you are ready, place both feet back on the floor. Take a few cleansing breaths to complete the exercise.

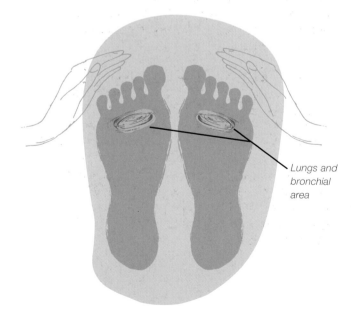

Lungs and bronchial area

Applying firm pressure on this area of the foot can help relieve congestion in the lungs.

Bronchial Opening

Origin: Western; guided imagery based on Western medicine and Eastern energy practices.

Objective: **To open bronchial passages**

Frequency of use: **Use as needed**

Duration: **10–15 minutes**

Cross-reference: **Use Abdominal Breathing (page 29) and Grounding (page 30)**

Difficulty level 2: **Requires ability to sustain concentration**

Complementary treatment: **Autogenic Training (page 54)**

1 Begin this meditation by familiarizing yourself with the respiratory system (see illustration on page 84). Choose your preferred sitting position. Close your eyes and engage in Abdominal Breathing...

2 Take a moment to establish a grounding connection with the earth...Trace the pathway of your breath. Draw in a breath of fresh air through your nose. Feel or see the air moving through the sinus cavities, the hollow spaces that serve to regulate the humidity and temperature of the air.

3 Feel the air traveling to your throat and downward into the windpipe...Try to feel the sensations of the air traveling downward...

4 The air moves through the windpipe to the lungs...then through the bronchial tubes, which lead to the right and left lobes of the lungs...

5 The bronchial tubes are lined with cilia, tiny hairs with a wavelike motion...The cilia wave as the air moves across them, acting as miniature brushes cleaning out dust and germs...These are collected in the mucus and then coughed up...

6 The bronchial tubes branch out into the right lung...The right lung has three lobes, each like a balloon filled with tiny sponges...Another bronchial tube branches to the left lung, which has two lobes...The oxygen inflates the balloonlike lobes...

7 The smallest branches of the bronchial tubes are called bronchioles...At the end of the bronchioles are tiny air sacs called alveoli, the end destination for the oxygen...Here the oxygen is absorbed into the bloodstream and exhaled as carbon dioxide...

8 Refocus on the air entering through your nose...Visualize a sky-blue color entering the air stream...Follow this crystal blue as it travels through the sinus cavities receiving moisture from the humidity...

9 The crystal blue travels down the throat and the windpipe to the bronchial tubes...The blue air moves over the cilia, cleansing any dust or germs...The blue air thins the mucus, making it easier to breathe...

continue →

Focusing on your bronchial tubes can help to improve conditions such as asthma.

10 The crystal blue branches out into the right and left lobes of the lungs...The blue soothes and cools the inflammation of the bronchial tubes... It allows the air to pass freely and smoothly through the branches of the bronchioles...

11 The crystal blue enters the tiny balloonlike sacs at the end of these branches...Each air sac expands fully, receiving the vital oxygen and sending it out into the bloodstream...

12 Repeat this cycle of blue light for 10–15 minutes. When you are ready, draw in a few cleansing breaths and open your eyes.

Voice box

Windpipe

Esophagus

Left main bronchial tube

Right main bronchial tube

Right lung

Left lung

High or Low Blood Pressure

The following meditations are outstanding for treating high or low blood pressure:

a) Rhythm of the Heart   b) Relax and Rejuvenate

Rhythm of the Heart

Origin: Western; guided imagery designed to help in slowing one's inner pace to achieve balance, thereby regulating blood pressure.

Objective: To relieve high or low blood pressure

Frequency of use: Can be done daily

Duration: 5–10 minutes

Cross-reference: Mudra of Knowledge (page 25) and Abdominal Breathing (page 29)

Difficulty level 2: Requires ability to sustain focus

Complementary treatment: Progressive Muscle Relaxation (page 46)

1 Choose your favorite meditation position. Close your eyes and place your hands in the Mudra of Knowledge position...Take a moment to get comfortable...Take a few deep-cleansing breaths...

2 Follow the natural rhythm of your breath... The breath ebbs and the breath flows... The abdomen rises and falls in a gentle dance rhythm...One beat goes up, one beat goes down...Up and down...Ebbing and flowing...

3 Your life is a dance that moves from moment to moment, step to step...What kind of dance would you describe your life as being?...A fast-paced dance like a foxtrot, rhythmic like a swing, or perhaps the lovely cadence of a waltz?...Your dance may change at different times. When you feel pressured, most likely the dance becomes quite fast.

4 Notice the rhythm of your life dance...Take your life dance and slow it down...Slow down the steps of your life so that you can watch and observe them...Step by step...Begin to feel the lovely cadence of a waltz...One, two, three...One, two, three...One, two, three...Feel the rhythmic sway of each step...Life is your dance partner...

5 As you reflect on your life's rhythm, insert pauses between one activity and the next... By taking the time to pause from one movement to the next, you begin to enjoy the process and release the obsession of constant motion...

6 Richness lies within each step of the path... In a dance, each step is important and each pause equally important...The dance cannot be performed without the mind, heart, and body moving together...Notice if you are in sync with the music that drives your life...Slow the dance steps...See yourself taking the time to pause and breathe throughout the activities of the day.

7 Ask your inner wisdom to show you how you may be out of sync with your life...Ask how to get in rhythm...Follow the rhythm of your breath as you listen...Imagine your heart beating out a perfectly timed rhythm...The body matches this rhythm...The mind partners the body and your actions reflect this rhythm in your daily life...

8 Return your attention to the natural flow of the breath...Count backward slowly from ten to one to come to waking consciousness..."Ten one-thousand...Nine one-thousand," etc...

Relax and Rejuvenate

Origin: Based on Western practices of relaxation to reduce stress and balance blood pressure.

🏃 **Objective: To treat high or low blood pressure**

🔄 **Frequency of use: Use daily or as needed**

🕐 **Duration: 10–15 minutes**

↔ **Cross-reference: Use Abdominal Breathing (page 29) and Open Palms (page 24)**

① **Difficulty level 1: Basic level of concentration needed**

🌿 **Complementary treatment: Autogenic Training (page 54)**

➕ **Quick remedy**

1 Choose your preferred meditation position... Close your eyes...Place your tongue on the roof of your mouth...Follow your breath with your mind.

2 Create a bright, warm, golden sun about 10 to 12 inches (25–30 cm) above your head...Direct this golden sun to release its radiant heat down through the top of your head into your body...

3 A wave of heat moves over your head, relaxing the muscles of the jaw and face...This warmth spreads down through your neck into your shoulders, encouraging them to drop and release any tension or tightness...The heat pours into your chest and upper back and radiates down the arms and out through your open palms...

4 Follow the breath as you go deeper and deeper into a state of relaxation...Waves of heat continue down into your abdomen, buttocks, and lower back, melting away stress...The waves reach all the way down your legs into the ankles and feet.

5 Feel how solid the ground is beneath you... Give your full weight over to the pull of gravity...

6 As you completely relax, draw inward to the silence...Move into a place of quiet reflection... Count down from ten to one, letting your mind choose how deep you want to go...Ten...Nine... Eight...Seven...Descend into a deeper relaxation... Six...Five...Four...Three...Two...One.

7 Begin to feel the soothing rhythm of your heartbeat...lub dub...lub dub...lub dub...Breathe in time to this rhythm...lub dub...lub dub...lub dub.

8 Feel the gentle movement and flow of this rhythm...Be concerned with nothing else except giving yourself over to this rhythm...Your entire body pulsates to this rhythm...As you flow with this rhythm you are lulled into a deeper and deeper state of relaxation...

9 Rest here in the rhythm of the heartbeat for as long as you choose...When you are ready to come to waking consciousness, count up from one to ten...One...Two...Three...Four...Feel refreshed and rejuvenated...Five...Six...Seven...Feel vibrant with energy...Eight...Nine...Ten...Take a moment to readjust to your external surroundings...

Inflammation-related Ailments

The following meditations are effective in reducing pain and stiffness in the joints:

a) Cooling the Fire   b) Ball of Chi

Cooling the Fire

Origin: Western; guided imagery to promote joint mobility.

🚶 **Objective: To relieve joint pain and stiffness**

⏱ **Frequency of use: Use as needed**

🕐 **Duration: 5–10 minutes**

↔ **Cross-reference: Use Observing the Breath (page 28)**

① **Difficulty level 1: Requires basic ability to sustain focus**

🍃 **Complementary treatment: Color Release (page 58)**

Depending on your needs, you can modify this exercise to decrease joint stiffness. Simply change the image of the icy blue ball of energy into a warm red ball of energy and follow the same steps

1 Choose your preferred sitting or reclining position. Close your eyes...Place your tongue on the roof of your mouth...Begin to follow the breath with your mind. Notice the natural rhythm of the inhalation and exhalation.

2 Create an icy blue ball of energy, 10–12 inches (25–30 cm) above your head...This ball contains healing, universal chi...As you focus on this blue ball, its healing properties become more concentrated...

3 On your next inhalation, draw this blue energy in through the top of your head as if you were sipping the energy through a plastic straw...The blue energy enters your body and flows in like soothing, cool water...

4 Bring your focus to a joint in your body... Breathe the blue healing energy into this joint...The icy blue penetrates deeply into the joint...Take a few breaths into the joint area...The icy blue begins to cool the painful fires of inflammation.

5 Breathe space into the joint...The pain begins to lessen and dissipate, diminishing the swelling...

6 Move your attention to another sore joint and repeat the same steps...Continue until you have addressed each inflamed joint. When you are ready, release the icy blue image...Return your attention to your entire body and the simple inhalation and exhalation of your breath...Open your eyes and give yourself a moment to readjust.

Ball of Chi

Origin: Modified from Qi (Chi) Gong (pronounced chee gung), which is a meditative form of exercise from China. It teaches the practitioner to gather, direct, and shift chi (universal life force) to relieve arthritic inflammation and pain.

Objective: To relieve arthritic pain and increase joint mobility

Frequency of use: Use as needed

Duration: 7–10 minutes

Cross-reference: Use Abdominal Breathing (page 29) and Grounding (page 30)

Difficulty level 1: Technique is easily administered

Complementary treatment: Pain Release (page 59)

Quick remedy

1 Stand or sit with your feet about shoulder-width apart. Your feet connect with the yin or earth energy. As you work with your hands, you will gather yang or heaven energy.

2 Bring your hands up to chest level, palms facing each other. Bring your hands slowly together and apart...Perhaps you can feel a tingling sensation as your palms come closer. The energy may feel palpable like down feathers, or you may feel nothing at all. If you feel nothing, simply pretend. The important thing is your intention to move and direct this subtle energy.

3 Now raise your arms, reaching toward heaven. Gather the heaven chi into your arms and hands...Bring them down in front of your heart...Form this heaven energy into a ball of warm light. Reach your arms up and gather more chi. Do this several times to strengthen and concentrate this energy.

4 Focus your breath on this ball of light...As you breathe in and out, imagine intensifying this yang energy...Now move the ball with your hands to an arthritic joint. (If it is a finger joint, use just one hand to direct the energy ball.)

5 Hold the energy ball over the joint and focus on your breath. With each inhalation and exhalation, imagine energy pulsating from your hands to the joint, the healing energy transferring from your palms to permeate the joint. Continue to hold your hands over this joint while focusing on your breath for a minute or so.

6 Direct this ball of chi to other joints in need of assistance. Repeat the same steps.

7 When you have completed this exercise, shake your hands out to release the heaven chi and any energetic residue you may have collected from the joints.

Digestive Disorders

The following techniques support healthy digestion:

a) Spinal Twists

b) Sun of Stomach

Spinal Twists

Origin: A commonly used yoga posture that activates the solar plexus chakra, thought to control digestion.

Ⓚ **Objective: To aid healthy digestion**

Ⓢ **Frequency of use: Use as needed**

Ⓞ **Duration: Hold each pose for 2–3 minutes, repeating as necessary**

↔ **Cross-reference: Use Observing the Breath (page 28)**

① **Difficulty level 1: Easy to administer and requires minimal flexibility**

Ⓛ **Complementary treatment: Autogenic Training (page 54)**

⊕ **Quick remedy**

Seated Spinal Twist

1 Begin in a comfortable sitting position on a floor mat. Extend both legs straight out in front of you with your back erect (you may bend your knees if necessary).

2 Grab the back of your right knee with your hands. Bend your knee and draw it up close to your body, bringing the heel of your foot toward your buttocks...Take a few deep breaths.

3 Place your hands around the front of your right knee. Wrap your left arm around your knee so that the inside of the elbow cradles the knee. Take your right hand and grab your left wrist...

4 Breathe in and lift your chest...Gently begin to twist your chest and shoulders to the right. Twist as far as you comfortably can and stop right at the edge of discomfort...Hold and breathe in for 15–30 seconds...Release your hands and allow yourself to gently unwind out of the twist.

5 Repeat the same steps for the left side, again holding the pose for 15–30 seconds. Repeat three times, alternating from a right twist to a left twist.

Lying Spinal Twist

You can do this twist on a mat or towel on the floor or on your bed.

1 Lie on your back on the floor or bed. Stretch your legs out straight in front of you...Arms are relaxed by your side.

2 Draw the right foot toward you and place it next to your left knee, which stays flat on the surface. Extend your arms out from the shoulders to form a "T" shape. Lift your buttocks and shift your hips a few inches to the right and rest flat again...Drop your right knee across your left leg toward the floor. This will create a twist and gently stretch the spine.

3 Take a few cleansing breaths...Try to keep the shoulders flat or dropped toward the floor...If it is comfortable, allow the head to drop toward the right. Bring your focus to abdominal breathing and take slow, cleansing breaths. Hold the twist for 30–60 seconds. As you are twisting, your internal organs receive a massage that tones the digestive energies.

4 Untwist by turning your head straight and bringing your right knee up so that the foot rests on the flat surface. Square your hips by lifting and moving your buttocks a couple of inches to the left. Replace your right leg out straight next to your left leg. Now repeat the stretch on the other side.

5 Untwist by turning your head straight and bringing your left knee upward to rest the foot flat again. Square your hips by moving your buttocks a couple of inches to the right.

6 Roll over to your right side. Slowly and gently push yourself up with both your hands.

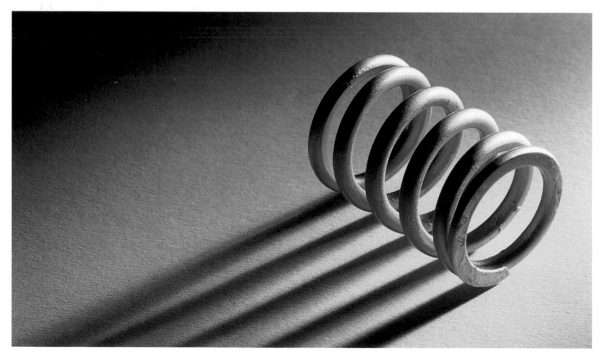

Sun of Stomach

Origin: Combined imagery from Hindu chakra practices used to activate third chakra to aid in digestion.

Objective: To aid in digestion

Frequency of use: Use as needed

Duration: 5–10 minutes

Cross-reference: Use Abdominal Breathing (page 29)

Difficulty level 1: Requires basic ability to sustain concentration

Complementary treatment: Chakra Cleansing and Balancing (page 34)

Quick remedy

1 The third chakra at the solar plexus is also known as the "sun of the stomach." Digestion is governed by this center. Wellness here is usually associated with the color yellow.

2 Choose your favorite sitting position. Close your eyes and place your tongue on the roof of your mouth. Anchor your mind to the breath.

3 Begin to draw the earth energy upward like an underground spring...This yin energy flows into the bottom of your feet and up into your legs. Feel the energy flowing steadily as it moves up into your groin and lower belly.

4 The earth chi flows upward to rest in the third chakra, located at the solar plexus... The earth energy gathers and fills this reservoir.

5 Turn your attention to the crown of your head... Visualize a bright golden sun. The breath gathers the heaven chi...it draws the chi in and directs it downward to the solar plexus...Here in the solar plexus the yin and yang, earth and heaven, energies mix in a complementary balance...Focus on a rich canary yellow...

6 Breathe into this canary yellow, intensifying its concentration...Direct this rich color to spread throughout your entire stomach area...The warmth moves outward to provide a soothing coat to the lining of the stomach and release any tension from this center.

7 Focus on the canary yellow for up to 10 minutes... When you are ready, release the color and open your eyes.

3

Enhancing Techniques

Anger Management

The following meditations offer different approaches to addressing anger:

a) Diffuse and Discharge   b) Shift Your Perceptions   c) Healthy Expression

Diffuse and Discharge

Origin: Combined imagery from Eastern principles of Ayurveda and Chi Gong to diffuse excessive energy from the body.

⚘ **Objective: To release anger**

⟳ **Frequency of use: May be used as needed**

◔ **Duration: Sustain practice for 3–5 minutes**

↔ **Cross-reference: Use Abdominal Breathing (page 29)**

① **Difficulty level 1: Technique is easily achieved**

⊘ **Complementary treatment: Autogenic Training (page 54)**

⊕ **Quick remedy**

If you still feel considerably angry after this meditation, you may wish to engage in a more physically demanding exercise, such as vigorous walking or cycling. As an alternative, try one of the techniques for managing anger that follow this exercise.

1 Sit on the floor in a comfortable, cross-legged position.

2 Notice your breathing. Is it faster than normal?...How deep is your breathing at this moment?...Notice your anger and where you feel it in your body....Breathe into the anger...

3 If your anger were a color, what color would it be?...Naming the color of the anger turns it into an energy form...See that color in your body...Breathe into that color...

4 Place the palms of your hands flat on the floor, either to your sides or in front of you...Take a deep breath...As you exhale, send that color into the earth, discharging and releasing it...

5 Vigorously press your palms into the floor. This helps to give a physical release...Direct the anger downward into the earth...The earth absorbs the anger and recycles it into neutral energy...Continue to breathe and discharge your anger, letting it flow out of your body like water going down a drain...

6 When you feel ready, release your palms...Sit upright...Begin to focus on the simple inhalation and exhalation of your breath...

7 When you are ready, stand up and take a moment to readjust.

Shift Your Perceptions

Origin: Guided imagery based on Western psychology.

🧍 **Objective: To treat excessive/chronic anger**

🕐 **Frequency of use: May be used daily**

🕐 **Duration: Sustain practice for at least 20 minutes**

↔ **Cross-reference: Use Open Palms (page 24) and Counting the Breath (page 27)**

① **Difficulty level 1: Technique is easily achieved**

🍃 **Complementary treatment: Progressive Muscle Relaxation (page 46)**

⊕ **Quick remedy**

The technique of enveloping yourself in an energy bubble helps to create a safe container for you to experience your feelings and is also a great tool for creating everyday boundaries.

1 Choose your preferred meditation position. Close your eyes and engage in Observing the Breath.

2 Bring to mind a situation you are angry about...This may be from the past or the present.

3 Focus on the circumstances that led to the anger...If it is in the past, recreate the scene in your mind....What transpired to trigger your anger?...When did you first notice your anger?...Did the anger arise slowly over time or did it ignite quickly?

4 Begin to notice the self-talk and beliefs you have in relation to this anger...Be as observant and as honest with yourself as possible...Try to identify what distortion lies within that particular thought...What might you be gaining from staying attached to this thought?...Is there another way to look at this?...Can you broaden your perspective?

5 Create a bubble of light around your body...See yourself resting in this egg-shaped bubble...The light radiates equally above your head, below your feet, on either side of you, in front and behind you.

6 This bubble is a safe container in which you can experience your feelings. Begin to focus on your feelings of anger rather than your angry thoughts. Notice where you feel the anger in your body. Breathe into this anger...Give yourself permission simply to experience the anger rather than engaging in the accompanying thoughts. Own your angry feelings in your body rather than focusing the blame on another person. Simply feel the anger as you breathe into it.

7 If the anger were a color, what color would it be? Breathe into this color, allowing it to diffuse the anger...The anger colors move out into the bubble...The color evaporates into a smoke that fills the bubble.

8 Focus on your grounding cord, expanding it to encompass the radius of the bubble...Begin to direct and release the smoke down your grounding cord into the earth...

9 Continue to focus on your breath and release the anger into the earth. When you are ready, return your focus to the simple inhalation and exhalation of the breath...If you like, you can keep this bubble around you or simply dissolve it...Open your eyes and take a moment to readjust.

Healthy Expression

Origin: Psychology and guided imagery used to promote healthy expression of emotions.

(人) **Objective: Healthy expression of anger**

(⑤) **Frequency of use: Use as needed**

(◎) **Duration: Sustain for 10–15 minutes, as required**

(↔) **Cross-reference: Use Abdominal Breathing (page 29)**

(①) **Difficulty level 2: Requires ability to sustain focus**

(∅) **Complementary treatment: Shift Your Perceptions (page 95)**

This meditation involves doing a mental rehearsal. You will need a piece of paper and a pen or pencil next to you.

1 Choose your favorite sitting position. Close your eyes...Place your tongue on the roof of your mouth...Inhale through your nose and focus on Abdominal Breathing.

2 When you feel sufficiently centered and relaxed, choose a scenario in which you would like to express your anger to someone. This may be a current situation or a past one. Have you somehow become detached from this anger or is the anger still strong?

3 Take a moment to define the factors that contributed to your anger...Were your feelings hurt?...Did you feel discounted or dismissed?...Was a boundary or personal value violated?...Try to be as specific as possible about how you feel. Write this down.

4 What were the actions, words, or behaviors that made you angry? Write them down.

5 What do you need from this person to rectify this or future behavior?...Don't be concerned about whether or not he will be able to meet this need...Simply write it down.

6 Close your eyes...Imagine that this person is sitting across from you...He is willing to listen and hear what you have to say...You are completely safe to express your feelings...

7 As you speak, use "I" statements. This allows you to take responsibility for your feelings rather than blaming the other person. Begin by telling the offender the specific behavior that upset you. For example, "I feel angry because you were an hour late for our appointment"..."When you did ___ I felt hurt and angry"...or..."When you speak in that tone I feel disrespected." Keep your communication simple and precise. See the person listening and receiving your communication...As you are speaking, notice how you feel and any sensations that arise within.

8 Ask the person to fulfill a specific need, such as, "It will help me if you ask for my help rather than give me an order." Then ask the person if he feels this is something he can do. If not, perhaps you can negotiate a compromise.

9 Return your attention toward yourself, allowing this person to disappear. Focus on your breath and notice any sensations that may have shifted during this mental rehearsal. When you are ready, open your eyes...Take a few deep-cleansing breaths and give yourself time to readjust.

Depression

Depression seems to be nature's way of pulling us inward to a place of reflection and introspection. While we all experience sadness from time to time, depression is a continued state of sadness often triggered by a major event such as a significant change, loss, or death of a loved one. Depression can also be related to unresolved emotional issues or the result of innumerable small losses and disappointments accumulated over a lifetime. We frequently become depressed when we feel as if we are unable to move forward or have no good viable options for the immediate or long-term future.

Clinical depression, however, is a serious condition. Seek medical attention if you have five or more of the following symptoms for two weeks or longer:

- Depressed mood, feeling sad or empty for most of the day, nearly every day.
- Noticeably diminished interest or pleasure in all, or almost all, activities nearly every day.
- Significant weight loss when not dieting, or weight gain.
- Insomnia or excessive sleep nearly every day.
- Feelings of restlessness or being slowed down.
- Fatigue or energy loss nearly every day.
- Feelings of worthlessness or inappropriate guilt nearly every day.
- Difficulty concentrating or indecisiveness nearly every day.
- Recurrent thoughts of death or suicide, suicide attempt, or specific plans for committing suicide.

If you have clinical depression, the following treatments should be used only with the consent of a doctor.

Situational Depression

The following meditations are excellent for addressing depression:

a) Opening the Heart   b) Grieving Loss Due to Death   c) Chest Opener

Opening the Heart

Origin: Combined from Western and Eastern mystical practices to energetically open the heart center and relieve depressive symptoms.

Objective: To assist in healing situational depression

Frequency of use: Recommended up to every other day to effect change

Duration: Sustain for 10–15 minutes or as long as comfortable

Cross-reference: Use Open Palms (page 24) and Observing the Breath (page 28)

Difficulty level 1: Technique requires willingness to explore emotions

Complementary treatment: Compassionate Heart (page 113)

1 Begin in your preferred sitting or reclining meditation position. Close your eyes...Engage in Observing the Breath...

2 Hold the image of someone you love in your mind's eye, someone who extends unconditional, positive regard to you. Invoke that person's loving presence...Hold his hand...What feelings or sensations arise within you as you think of this loved one? Notice how he naturally wants to reach out to comfort you.

3 Gently place your hands palms down over the heart center, located at the sternum...Breathe freely and naturally, allowing the breath to gently permeate your heart...Feel your heart beating beneath your hands...Notice if you have been guarding your heart recently...

4 Appreciate the importance of your heart, both physically and emotionally...Are there any areas in your heart or life that have become emotionally closed off or hardened?...Allow yourself to explore these places gently...

5 Guide the breath to enter these places...Extend a gentle caring that softens the hardness... The breath opens an exquisite heart flower, petal by petal...Be open to the feelings that begin to surface, letting go of any need to protect yourself...Here in the presence of your loved one it is safe to feel...His love gives you the courage to embrace this stream of emotional energy...

6 There may also be places within your heart that are overflowing with sadness and grief. This may feel overwhelming, like a mighty river that may drown you...Go with this flow...The intensity of the sadness, like the pace of the river, will not continue at this level...With time and acceptance it will run its course...The more quickly you allow for the flow of emotions, the more quickly your heart will heal.

7 When you are ready...Thank your loved one for his presence...Turn your attention from your heart, dropping your hands in your lap...Focus on your breath...Slowly open your eyes...Take a few moments to readjust...You may require a brief resting period...

Grieving Loss Due to Death

Origin: Guided imagery based on Western psychology to promote healing due to grief.

Objective: To alleviate depression due to bereavement

Difficulty level 1: Technique requires willingness to explore emotions

Frequency of use: May be used periodically

Complementary treatment: Compassionate Heart (page 113)

Duration: Sustain practice for 10–15 minutes

Cross-reference: Use Open Palms (page 24) and Abdominal Breathing (page 29)

1 Choose your preferred sitting or reclining position. Close your eyes...Engage in Abdominal Breathing...

2 Begin to follow the natural rhythm of the breath...In and out...The breath ebbs and flows like the waves hitting the shore...Move with the rhythm as if you were the waves approaching and receding from the shoreline...In and out...Ebbing and flowing...The rhythm brings you to a place within where no time and space exist, just the movement of the breath.

3 The breath becomes a gentle breeze that lifts you and carries you through a hidden doorway in your heart...The breeze gently places you in a lush field of green...Notice the trees at the edge of a lovely forest...Begin to walk toward the forest...

4 As you reach the forest, enter through its canopy of trees...These trees are ancient... They have lived for hundreds of years and have witnessed much...As you walk through the forest, your senses are deeply awakened...Take in the many delightful sights...The forest is alive with wonderful sounds...Feel pine needles like a soft blanket cushioning your feet as you stroll along...

5 In time you come upon the most beautiful grandfather tree you have ever seen...You reach out to touch the bark and feel love radiating from the tree's core...Embrace the tree, wrapping your arms as far around it as possible...

6 Breathe in and feel the fullness of your sadness...As you exhale, release the depth of your sadness into the tree...As you lean into this tree you seem to enter the tree and become part of its inner wood...

7 The center of the tree is filled with a light that carries you upward into the tree limbs...Here you magically enter a magnificent bird...The bird takes off in flight, soaring high above the forest...

8 From the bird's eye, you can see vast expanses below you...The bird dives back, landing on a big rock in a different part of the forest...

continue →

9 Breathe in the beauty of this place...Feel the presence of another living being approaching from the distance...There is a person walking toward you...It is your loved one...You can hardly believe what you see at first...Then you reach out and touch them, filled with joy at your reunion...Hold hands and sit together for a while...You may have many questions...Take your time to exchange communication...Say whatever is in your heart...

10 When you sense it is time to leave, say your words of parting, knowing with confidence you will see each other again...

11 Spot another path that brings you back to the lush field of green...Here a warm and gentle breeze lifts you and carries you back through the doorway in your heart.

12 Become aware once again of the sound of the ocean waves...Feel the inhalation and exhalation of your breath...Slowly counting backward from ten, return to waking consciousness...Ten...Nine...Eight...

Chest Opener

Origin: Iyengar yoga practices thought to activate and open the heart center and relieve depressive symptoms.

(人) **Objective: To aid in healing chronic depression**

(⟳) **Frequency of use: May be used daily**

(⏱) **Duration: Practice for 1–5 minutes or longer**

(↔) **Cross-reference: Use Abdominal Breathing (page 29)**

(1) **Difficulty level 1: Technique is easy and quite effective with practice**

(✿) **Complementary treatment: Opening the Heart (page 98)**

(+) **Quick remedy**

You will need two or three blankets. Fold each one in half, then roll it into a cylindrical shape. Place them on top of each other on the floor (or if this is uncomfortable on a bed). When you lie across these blankets you should feel comfortable, with no pressure or strain on your back or neck. Adjust the height of the blankets as necessary.

1 Sit on the floor in front of the bolster of blankets. Reach your hands back on either side of the blankets...Begin to bend your elbows to gently lower your back and recline fully over the blankets. The blankets should touch about midway down your shoulder blade.

2 Allow your neck and shoulders to rest comfortably on the floor...If this puts a strain on them, place a small pillow under your head.

3 Extend your feet out in front of you...Allow your arms to extend out from your shoulders directly to the side, forming a "T" shape.

4 Close your eyes...Take a deep breath in and exhale slowly...Repeat...Concentrate on breathing into the muscles across your chest and upper back...Your muscles may feel tight as you first enter this pose...Simply acknowledge whatever sensations arise by breathing into them...

5 Allow the muscles of the neck and throat to soften and open gently...Breathe into this opening as you feel yourself relax more fully into this pose...

6 Return your focus to your chest area... The sensations of opening the chest may feel unfamiliar or awkward. Opening and exposing your chest and abdominal muscles may make you feel vulnerable at first...Try to stay with this openness...

7 Direct your attention to your heart center, located at the sternum...Breathe into your heart...Soften any feelings of tightness or closed space...Focus on the simple inhalation and exhalation as it gently begins to create a sense of inner space...

8 The breath carries a color of green to the heart...Perhaps it is the lush green of a field or a spring leaf...The green light enters your heart, washing away any past hurt and sadness you are ready to release...

9 Stay here as long as you wish...Then return your attention to the gentle ebb and flow of your breath...Come out of the pose by bending your knees and rolling over to your right side, using both hands to push yourself upright.

Worry, Anxiety, Fear

The following meditations address worry, anxiety, and fear:

a) Transforming Fear   b) Reframing Thoughts   c) Practice of Sending and Receiving

Transforming Fear

Origin: Derived from Eastern and esoteric Christian practices. Used to lift fear from the solar plexus center to the heart center to transform fear.

⊛ **Objective: To transform fear**

⟳ **Frequency of use: May be used daily or as needed**

⊘ **Duration: Sustain practice for 10–15 minutes**

⟷ **Cross-reference: Use Open Palms (page 24) and Abdominal Breathing (page 29)**

① **Difficulty level 1: Easy to administer**

⊘ **Complementary treatment: Reframing Thoughts (page 103)**

⊕ **Quick remedy**

1 Begin in your preferred sitting or reclining position. Close your eyes...Engage in Abdominal Breathing.

2 Bring to mind a fear you are grappling with... Perhaps this is an ongoing fear or a fear regarding the future...

3 Focus on your thoughts and emotions surrounding this fear...Are you aware of what initially triggered this fear?...Did it arise quickly or build over time?...Is the fear specific?... Or is it a feeling of general apprehension?...Focus on where you feel the fear in your body...Breathe into that area...

4 Place your hands over your solar plexus, just below the sternum...If the fear were a color, what color would it be? Direct the color into the third energy center, located at the solar plexus...This center acts like a sponge, absorbing the color.

5 Ask yourself, "What am I most afraid about? What is the worst-case scenario?"...Listen with kind interest...

6 Place your left hand over your heart center while keeping the right hand over the solar plexus...Direct the fear from your solar plexus to your heart center...See the fear rising like a smoky mist into your heart...Give your worries, anxieties, and fears over to your heart...

7 Breathe into your heart center...creating space to accept and transform the fear...Feel the heart embrace what it receives, absorbing the fear into the greater whole...

8 Imagine a person or symbol that represents the qualities of courage, compassion, and humility... Invoke those qualities...Accept this loving-kindness into your heart...Feel the fear transforming...Perhaps to courage or acceptance or knowledge.

9 The energy of fear transforms into a new color in the heart...Breathe into that color and imagine it radiating throughout and beyond your body into the space around you...Here in this bubble you are encased in the courage of the heart.

10 When you are ready, slowly open your eyes and take a few moments to readjust.

Reframing Thoughts

Origin: Combined approach utilizing Western mysticism and psychology to reframe negative thoughts into positive ones, thereby reducing anxiety.

Objective: To aid in overcoming worry and anxiety

Frequency of use: May be used as needed

Duration: Sustain practice for 10–15 minutes

Cross-reference: Use Mudra of Knowledge (page 25) and Abdominal Breathing (page 29)

Difficulty level 1: Minimal level of concentration needed

Complementary treatment: Transforming Fear (page 102)

Quick remedy

1 Choose your preferred meditation position... Close your eyes, place your tongue behind your upper teeth, and engage in Abdominal Breathing...

2 The breath disengages the mind and brings its focus to the present moment...Keep your mind focused...Simply watch as sensations arise and fall away...Feel your connection to your body, to your emotions, and to your mind...

3 Center yourself in your mind...See a brilliant white light radiating from your mind...This is the light of clear reason...

4 Create a bubble out in front of you...Choose a fearful or negative thought to examine...Place the thought and any fear surrounding the thought into the bubble...Focus the light onto this thought... This light illuminates any emotions, beliefs, and personal meanings attached to this thought...

5 Consider how this thought influences your actions and reactions...How has this thought served you up until this moment?...What are the costs and benefits of maintaining this belief?

6 Breathe into this thought...Ask that this thought be infused with light and new understanding...You have the power to change this thought if you choose...

7 Release the bubble like a helium balloon... Give it over to the universal consciousness...

8 Create a new bubble...Choose a positive thought or coping statement to replace the fear, such as "This is not truth; it is simply a fear" or "I will cope with what arises in the future at that time." Place this new thought into the bubble...

9 Make that new thought real...Imagine what it would feel like to be released from this fear... Imagine how it would feel, physically and emotionally.

10 Place the bubble above your head...Pop the bubble and let the positive energy flow down into your body.

11 When you are ready, return your attention to the simple rhythm of the breath...Open your eyes and readjust.

Practice of Sending and Receiving

Origin: The practice of "Sending and Receiving" is also known as Tonglen meditation, a Tibetan Buddhist practice that cultivates compassion and fearlessness.

🧍 **Objective: To cultivate fearlessness**

🕐 **Frequency of use: May be used daily**

🕐 **Duration: Sustain practice for at least 10–15 minutes**

↔ **Cross-reference: Use Cupped Hands (page 25)**

① **Difficulty level 2: Technique requires ability to sustain concentration**

🍃 **Complementary treatment: Transforming Fear (page 102)**

The Practice of Sending and Receiving takes skill and emotional openness. Over time, you will expand your capacity to fully take in fear, or any other type of pain, and release compassion.

1 Begin in your preferred meditation position. Close your eyes...Place your tongue on the roof of your mouth...Take a deep breath and exhale slowly. Repeat several times, releasing any tension from your body...Follow the rhythm of your breath and the gentle rise and fall of your abdomen...

2 Be mindful of your breath...Watch as the breath comes and goes, ever fresh and changing... Notice the sensations that arise and fall away...Note the impermanence of the breath...It is here and it is gone...But it returns again in a never-ending circle...

3 Visualize the vast expanse of a blue sky on a cloudless day...Touch that blue for just a moment, then let it go...The vastness of the blue reminds us that the mind, too, has the ability to expand to openness...You are not your thoughts...

4 Bring a fear to mind...Give it a color, perhaps a deep, smoky black...Feel the heaviness and weight of the blackness...Breathe into the fear... Breathe it through all the pores of your body...

5 Breathe out the qualities of spaciousness... Open, free, light, perhaps the white silver color of moonlight...Breathe out the courage to be free from fear...

6 Breathe in the pain of fear...Breathe out the pleasure of love and compassion...Give the inhalation and exhalation equal measure...Continue this synchronization of the breath...

7 When you are ready, release the images you have been working with...Return your attention to the simple inhalation and exhalation of the breath...Open your eyes and take a moment to readjust.

Confidence/Self-esteem

The following meditations help build confidence and self-esteem:

a) Self-acceptance — Letting Go of Perfectionism　　b) Reclaiming Your Inner Child

c) Modified Virasana Pose

Self-acceptance — Letting Go of Perfectionism

Origin: Guided imagery based on Western psychology to promote self-acceptance and build confidence and self-esteem.

Objective: **To build confidence through self-acceptance**

Frequency of use: **Use regularly when feeling bound by perfection**

Duration: **Sustain practice for at least 7–10 minutes**

Cross-reference: **Use Open Palms (page 24) and Abdominal Breathing (page 29)**

Difficulty level 2: **Requires ability to sustain concentration**

Complementary treatment: **Challenging the Inner Critic (page 112)**

1 Choose your preferred meditation position. Close your eyes...Place your tongue on the roof of your mouth...Follow the natural rhythm of the breath as you engage in Abdominal Breathing.

2 Acknowledge the role of your heart as a symbol of love and wisdom...Acknowledge the role of your mind as a symbol of precision and possibilities... Reflect for a moment on which you tend to consult for guidance and decision making...Which aspect is more dominant?

3 Imagine a line of energy connecting your heart and your mind...Breathe into the line, expanding it into a beautiful footbridge...This bridge allows the heart and mind to exchange information...

4 Imagine the heart and mind working together... The heart tempers the mind with compassion... The mind tempers the heart with reason...

5 Reflect on a personal or professional ideal or standard that you hold dear...Consider the heart and mind playing equal roles in achieving this goal... Honor the precision and direction of the mind...Honor the vast internal resources that prompt you to achieve your ideals...Honor the compassion of the heart...The heart embraces your humanity and your limitations... The heart supports your pursuit of excellence but reminds you to honor your needs and limits...

6 Imagine that, working together, the heart and mind propel you to excel within your limits... Achieving through balance allows you to surpass what you could ever accomplish under the sole direction of the heart or mind.

7 See yourself sitting on this footbridge...Feel the energies of both the heart and mind solidly supporting you...Breathe in deeply, filling your soul with the breath of life...Here, in this instant, accept yourself for who you are...Accept all of who you are to the best of your ability...Accept your strengths and weaknesses...Accept them with humility rather than pride...Humility is realistic knowledge and acceptance of yourself for who you are now... Humility is a form of strength.

8 Feel the energy of the heart and mind sending you kindness and caring...Accept this into the entirety of who you are...

9 In an affirmation of your true self, close your meditation by silently sounding "Om....Om....Om" (pronounced "home" without the h)...Return to waking consciousness and take a moment to readjust to your surroundings.

Reclaiming Your Inner Child

Origin: Western psychological approach based on the work of counselor and theologian John Bradshaw.

Ⓧ **Objective: To instill self-confidence**

Ⓢ **Frequency of use: Use periodically to connect with your younger emotional self**

Ⓞ **Duration: Sustain practice for 15–20 minutes**

↔ **Cross-reference: Use Open Palms (page 24) and Grounding (page 30)**

① **Difficulty level 2: Requires ability to sustain concentration**

⊘ **Complementary treatment: Compassionate Heart (page 113)**

1 Choose your preferred meditation position. Close your eyes; place your tongue on the roof of your mouth. Take a few deep-cleansing breaths to release any tension from your body. Send grounding roots down from your soles into the earth.

2 Feel the roots reaching deeper and deeper into the earth with each breath. Feel the weight and heaviness of your body giving itself over to the strong force of gravity. Count to ten slowly..."One one-thousand...Two one-thousand..." Nothing exists but the ebb and flow of your breath.

3 A gentle breeze lifts you up and carries you back in time...Watch as the days of the calendar move backward...You find yourself in front of an old house...

4 Walk toward the front door...It is open...Move through the doorway and notice a door at the end of a hallway...Move down the hall toward this door...The door is locked...Remember a key inside your pocket...Place the key in the lock...It easily turns...Stand just inside the door of the room...

5 Discover a child inside...The child is not yet aware of your presence...As you observe this child, you realize the child is in fact you at a younger age...Notice the child...Notice his clothing...Notice what activity he is engaged in...Notice his mood and temperament...

6 Ponder if there is anything that has kept this child from feeling completely loved, understood, safe, and happy at this particular age...Quietly watch, hoping to glean insight...

7 The child slowly becomes aware of your presence...He is happy, perhaps relieved to see you, although a bit shy or wary...Introduce yourself and tell your younger self that you are here to bring him back into your life...Ask the child if you can come and sit next to him...

8 Let your child know that you arrived as soon as you could, and that you're sorry if he had to wait and wonder for a long while...Let the child know you want to be friends...

9 Sense the child beginning to trust you...Open your arms and tenderly invite the child to come closer...Wrap your child safely in your arms, rocking back and forth, expressing how much you care...You will listen to anything he wants to express...Ask if there is anything, anything at all, the child wants or needs from you...Listen and promise to give this to him as soon as possible...

10 Some time passes...Take your child by the hand and tell him you would like him to come and live with you...Take a last look around the room, close the door, and walk down the hallway back to the front door.

11 Exit the house and find you and your child being lifted, carried back upon the breeze to your body...

12 Focus on the ebb and flow of your breath...Sense the presence of your child nearby...He can now be included in your life for you to provide for any needs that were previously unmet.

13 Bring yourself back to waking consciousness by slowly counting back from ten to one... Open your eyes and take a moment to adjust to your external surroundings.

Modified Virasana Pose

Origin: Virasana is a yoga pose meaning "hero." It is the pose of courage and self-confidence that gently opens the heart energy to self-expression.

(✦) **Objective: To cultivate confidence/self-esteem**

(⟳) **Frequency of use: May be used daily or as needed**

(◷) **Duration: Sustain practice for 1–5 minutes**

(↔) **Cross-reference: Use Abdominal Breathing (page 29)**

(①) **Difficulty level 1: Technique is easily achieved**

(✎) **Complementary treatment: Shifting your Point of View (page 110)**

(✛) **Quick remedy**

Virasana means "hero." It is the yoga pose of courage and self-confidence. Lack of confidence and self-esteem is often associated with closed heart energy. The Virasana Pose gently opens the heart energy to self-expression.

For this pose you will need one or two folded blankets.

1 Sit on the blankets in a comfortable cross-legged position...Close your eyes...Place your tongue on the roof of your mouth...Anchor your mind to the breath, following its natural rhythm...

2 The breath pulls you inward to a place free from the demands of everyday living...Come to rest in this quiet place of reflection...Reflect upon a situation or area in your life in which you lack confidence...Notice any thoughts or emotions associated with this...Where in your body do you notice reactions?

3 Direct your attention to your heart center, located at the sternum...Imagine a symbol of courage and confidence...Feel the power of

that symbol resonating in your heart...Feel the strength of the courage radiating throughout your body...See yourself able to address the situation with confidence and calm certainty...

4 Inhale and raise your arms out to your side at shoulder height...Exhale and sweep your arms up over your head, interlocking your fingers and turning your palms toward the ceiling...

5 Release on the out-breath, sweeping your arms downward in a smooth, continual motion as if your hands were moving through water...

6 Reach your hands behind your buttocks and interlock your fingers...Be careful not to roll your shoulders forward...Squeeze your shoulder blades together to open your chest... At the same time, try to widen the muscles across your back, creating space between your shoulder blades...

7 Inhale deeply...Lift and open your chest like a proud warrior, activating the heart center...

4

8 Inhale and exhale for eight cycles, holding your image of courage and confidence firmly in your mind...(In time, you can extend holding this pose for up to five minutes.)

9 Affirm your courage by sounding the Om three times (pronounced "home" without the h), out loud or softly...

10 To come out of this pose, release your hands...Gently rise up on your knees, then sit back in your simple cross-legged position...SStretch your legs out in front of you with bent knees...Gently bounce your knees up and down on the floor to release any tension that may have gathered.

6

Shyness/Sensitivity

The Internet is a good source of information on classes to help shy individuals develop social skills. The following meditations help to overcome shyness/sensitivity:

a) Shifting Your Point of View   b) Separation Rose   c) Challenging The Inner Critic

Shifting Your Point of View

Origin: Combination of Western mysticism energy techniques.

Objective: To help overcome shyness

Frequency of use: May be used as needed

Duration: Sustain meditation for 10–15 minutes

Cross-reference: Use Counting the Breath (page 27) and Grounding Cord (page 41)

Difficulty level 1: Easy-to-follow guided imagery

Complementary treatment: Separation Rose (page 111)

Quick remedy

1 Choose your preferred meditation position. Close your eyes...Engage in Counting the Breath to relax and center yourself. Create your grounding cord.

2 Visualize a vast expanse of cobalt-blue sky on a cloudless day...Touch that blue with your mind for just a moment, then let it go...The vastness of the blue reminds you that the mind, too, has the ability to expand perceptions...You are not limited to your thoughts...

3 Bring to mind a social situation that fills you with fear...Imagine the uncomfortable bodily and emotional sensations that would arise...Breathe in deeply...As you exhale, direct the energy of the discomfort down your grounding cord and into the earth...

4 Release the energy of any preoccupation with your thoughts, feelings, or physical reactions...Let go of the need to perform or behave "perfectly."

5 Imagine you are surrounded by a beautifully colored bubble...This bubble gives you a sense of separation from the situation...In this bubble you are free to be who you are...You are free from

embarrassment...You can breathe and focus your attention on what the other person is saying...You are able to concentrate on the present moment without worrying about what you will say next...

6 See yourself behaving differently than you ever have before...See yourself interacting successfully...Allow the focus to be on others, taking comfort in the fact that most people love to talk about themselves...

7 Imagine that in the safety of this bubble you are calm, composed, and relaxed...If sensations of discomfort arise, simply acknowledge what you are feeling and release it down your grounding cord...You are in charge...You are free to reveal as much or as little about yourself as you choose...

8 As you leave this scenario, imagine feeling different than you have in the past...You walk away free from concern...This bubble is available to carry with you into any situation...Each time you practice, see yourself becoming more socially comfortable and competent...

9 Turn your attention once again to the simple inhalation and exhalation of the breath...Open your eyes...Give yourself a few moments to readjust.

Separation Rose

Origin: In Western esotericism the rose is a symbol of the soul much akin to the Eastern lotus flower that represents unfolding consciousness.

Objective: To aid in building confidence in social situations

Frequency of use: Best used regularly

Duration: Sustain for 10–15 minutes

Cross-reference: Use Abdominal Breathing (page 29) and Grounding Cord (page 41)

Difficulty level 2: Requires ability to sustain focus

Complementary treatment: Self-acceptance (page 105)

In Western esotericism, the rose is a symbol of the soul, much akin to the Eastern lotus flower that represents unfolding consciousness. The Separation Rose meditation is especially useful in helping shy individuals deflect a degree of sensitivity in social situations.

The first time you perform this meditation, you may wish to work with a real long-stemmed rose.

1 Choose your preferred meditation position. Close your eyes...Engage in Abdominal Breathing...

2 Imagine a golden light radiating from the heart center, located at the sternum...Feel the heat from the light fill your chest cavity and radiate throughout your entire body...

3 The light extends beyond your body to create an energetic bubble all around you...The light radiates equally above your head, below your feet, on either side of you, in front of you, and behind you.

4 This bubble is a safe container...Here within the bubble is your energy. Beyond the edge of the bubble is the world's energy...

5 Create the image of an exquisite long-stemmed rose...Make the rose the size of your body... Saturate the rose with color...Notice how full the petals are...Notice their velvety softness and the dew

drops pooling on them...Notice the thorns that protect the rose...Notice the texture of the leaves...

6 Place the rose on the very edge of your personal bubble...Give it a long stem capable of reaching down into the earth...

7 Feel the protective qualities of the rose...Enjoy resting in the energy of the bubble, separate from the stimulation of the external world...

8 Imagine yourself in a social situation...Your rose sits at the edge of your personal space...All the attention that is focused on you is deflected and absorbed into the rose...The rose's stem then directs the energy of this attention down the stem and releases it into the earth's soil...This allows you to stay separate from the external energies...You are free to focus on what the other person is saying and to express yourself easily...

9 See yourself carrying this rose with you wherever you go...If the rose becomes saturated with energy and begins to wilt, simply release that rose and create a fresh one...

10 When you are ready, return your attention to the rhythm of the breath...As you bring yourself to waking consciousness, keep your rose at the edge of your space...Practice carrying this rose with you throughout your day.

Challenging the Inner Critic

Origin: Psychology-oriented guided imagery to release critical tendencies and promote self-acceptance and expression.

(人) **Objective: To help alleviate shyness**

(⏱) **Frequency of use: May be used as needed**

(◎) **Duration: Sustain practice for 10–15 minutes**

(↔) **Cross-reference: Use Observing the Breath (page 28)**

(①) **Difficulty level 2: Requires ability to sustain concentration**

(◷) **Complementary treatment: Self-acceptance (page 105)**

1 Choose your preferred meditation position... Close your eyes...Engage in Observing the Breath...

2 Receive the fullness of the breath deep within your body...Allow the breath to bring cleansing and rejuvenation...If your mind wanders, return your attention to the breath...With each breath imagine that you are expanding your ability to accept yourself for who you are in this moment...

3 Call upon a symbol to represent your inner critic...Perhaps you see the critic as an animal, a person, a color...What qualities would you assign to your inner critic?

4 Invite the critic to join you for a conversation... Say hello and ask the critic how long it has been present with you...What has been its objective?...What is its greatest fear for you?... Perhaps it is the fear of rejection...Perhaps the critic understood when you were young that you were not allowed to have needs...The critic may have taught you perfectionism as a defense...

5 Honor the critic for trying to protect you... Thank it for serving you all these years... Bow in respect for its efforts...

6 Consider how you might update the critic's job to reflect your current needs more accurately... Perhaps the critic can continue to give advice but without harshness or condemnation...Perhaps the critic can become an advocate of discernment to guide you in making decisions...Perhaps the critic can help you assess the best approach to a situation. The critic may become a teacher in the refinement of tact and diplomacy.

7 You may choose any new qualities and roles for the critic to assume...Most importantly, the inner critic is to be a supportive rather than destructive commentator.

8 Thank the inner critic for participating in your conversation...Take a moment to reflect upon the meeting...

9 Return your attention to your breath and the gentle rise and fall of your abdomen...When you are ready, open your eyes and take time to readjust. When you become aware of the harsh voice of criticism, simply stop and acknowledge the information. Thank the critic for its concern. Breathe. Remind yourself and the inner critic of its new role and move on.

Compassion for Self and Others

The following meditations encourage compassion:

a) Compassionate Heart   b) Seed Thought Meditation

Compassionate Heart

Origin: Based on traditional Buddhist formal compassion practices.

(🏃) **Objective: To awaken and cultivate compassion**

(⟳) **Frequency of use: May be used regularly**

(◎) **Duration: Sustain practice for 15 minutes or more**

(↔) **Cross-reference: Use Open Palms (page 24) and Abdominal Breathing (page 29)**

(①) **Difficulty level 2: Requires ability to sustain concentration**

(🍃) **Complementary treatment: Opening the Heart (page 98)**

1 Choose your preferred sitting position. Place your hands in the Open Palms pose...Close your eyes...Place your tongue on the roof of your mouth and engage in Abdominal Breathing.

2 Begin by silently affirming that this practice is dedicated to the benefit of all sentient beings.

3 Direct your breath now to the heart center, located at the sternum...Raise your arms to chest level with your palms facing downward... Hold your hands here to gather the heart energy... A soft, white light glows steadily deep within your heart...A beautiful flower surrounds and encases this flame...The flame begins to grow stronger with each

3

4

breath...The petals of the flower open to reveal brilliant illumination...

4 Turn your hands over and bring your palms side by side at heart level...Feel warmth and comfort from the heart light...Hear and feel the words "I care" pumping through your heart...The energy of caring gently softens any places within the heart that have been closed or hardened by loss and sadness... These places unfold like an ethereal flower blooming with kindness...

5 Soften to whatever emotions or thoughts surface...Be patient...Let go of any need to protect yourself from past hurts that may have been locked away...Make space for whatever arises to be accepted without value or judgment... The love and compassion that lie within the heart bring forth courage...

6 Open your hands out to your sides, connecting with the universal energy...Open your heart to experience the sorrow and suffering of the world, including your own...Speak the words,

"May I be free from suffering and the root of suffering"...Breathe into the fullness of these words, keeping the openness in your heart...

7 Turn your attention to your neighbors and community by asking, "May my neighbors and community be free from suffering and the root of suffering"...Again, breathe into the fullness of these words, allowing the heart to remain open...

8 Lastly, awaken compassion for all beings throughout the universe by saying, "May all beings be free from suffering and the root of suffering"...Breathe into the universal pain of sorrow and suffering, making room in your heart to extend compassion to all beings, great and small...

9 Release these words by bringing your hands to the prayer position...Breathe deeply...In your preferred manner, give thanks for what you have experienced in the meditation...When you are ready, open your eyes and give yourself a good, long stretch...

Many religions and cultures include teachings about the importance of compassion toward others. Here are just a few examples.

Buddhism says: "Hurt not others in ways that you yourself would find harmful."— Udana-Varga 5.18.

Christianity instructs: "Whatever you wish men to do for you, do likewise also for them; for this is the law and the prophets."— Matthew 7.2.

Taoism proclaims: "Regard you neighbor's gain as your own gain and your neighbor's loss as your own loss."—T'ai Shang Kan Ying P'ien.

Seed Thought Meditation

Origin: Roots in the Judaic Kabbalah tradition, widely used in esoteric meditation and Agni yoga as a transcendent form of active meditation. The purpose is to pierce the veil that separates the lower mind from the higher mind to instill greater self-awareness.

Ⓧ **Objective: To deepen understanding of compassion**

Ⓢ **Frequency of use: Use once daily for three weeks, then as needed**

Ⓓ **Duration: Sustain practice for 10–20 minutes**

↔ **Cross-reference: Use Open Palms (page 24), Soulstar (page 122), Observing the Breath (page 28)**

① **Difficulty level 2: Requires ability to sustain concentration**

🌿 **Complementary treatment: Compassionate Heart (page 113)**

You will need a sheet of paper and a pen or pencil for this exercise. Before beginning the meditation, write the word "Compassion" in large letters with a space between each letter: C-O-M-P-A-S-S-I-O-N.

This meditation begins with the Soulstar. It is helpful to practice this meditation until you can recall it easily on your own. The Soulstar appears again later, in the section on "Trust" (page 122).

To obtain the most benefit, do this meditation daily for three weeks, recording your experiences in a journal. You may explore the qualities of any word by substituting it for compassion.

1 Choose your preferred sitting position. Close your eyes...Place your tongue on the roof of your mouth. Take a deep breath and exhale slowly.

2 Begin with the Soulstar meditation. Visualize a clear, white light 10–12 inches (25–30 cm) directly above your head. This is the Soulstar, the light of your High Self...As you focus on the light, it begins to expand...

3 Center yourself in the steadiness of this pure and loving light. On your next inhalation, draw this light down into your heart center, located at the sternum...Feel this light magnifying your feelings of caring...Move your attention to your mind...Postulate that you are lifting your consciousness from the lower mind to the higher mind...

4 Extend a line of light from the roof of your mouth upward to reach 10–12 inches (25–30 cm) above your head...This light forms a magnetized cloud of consciousness from which to focus on the seed thought...

5 Open your eyes...Look intently at the word on the paper for a few seconds, and then close your eyes. Mentally say, "I seek the meaning behind this word COMPASSION"...Focus inwardly on this word...

6 Place the word in the center of your mind. See it...Take it in...Mentally repeat the word several times...Let the word become a mantra... Hear it...Allow it to make an impression upon you...

7 Sense the vibration of the word...The vibration is the quality of the word...What qualities does compassion have?...Is it soft and giving?...Is it expansive and encompassing?...

8 Holding the word in your mind, focus your attention first upon one letter, then another... The seed thought expands until your mind can no longer contain the size of it...

9 Silently ask a series of questions...Pause after each one to receive any impressions into your conscious awareness...How do I experience this word?...How is COMPASSION expressed in the world?... What is the ultimate source of this word?... Why does this essence exist?...What is my next step in experiencing/expressing this essence in my daily life?...

10 Take all the time you need to ask these questions and listen for a response. If you wish, repeat any of the questions to try to penetrate the word more deeply.

11 As you ask these questions, seek to attune to the deepest meaning of this word...The knowledge may come as words, pictures, images, sounds, patterns, melodies, feelings, abstract symbols, impressions, even tastes and smells.

12 As you focus on this word, you are pressing your higher mind into the thought... Feel a sense of upward lifting...In turn, the word COMPASSION makes an impression upon your consciousness...

13 When you are ready...Release your focus on the seed thought...Let go of the symbol of the Soulstar...Return to the simple inhalation and exhalation of the breath...Take your time to open your eyes and readjust...Take a few minutes to write down the images, responses, and impressions you received from the meditation.

Relationships

The following meditations provide relationship support:

a) Clear Communication

b) Releasing Old Ties

Clear Communication

Origin: Blend of Eastern and Western energy practices designed to promote clear communication in interpersonal relationships.

Objective: To enhance clear communication

Frequency of use: May be used as needed

Duration: Sustain practice for approximately 10–15 minutes

Cross-reference: Use Cupped Hands (page 25) and Abdominal Breathing (page 29)

Difficulty level 2: Requires ability to sustain concentration

Complementary treatment: Mental Sponge (page 61)

1 Begin in your preferred sitting position...Close your eyes...Engage in Abdominal Breathing.

2 Consider an important personal or professional relationship that requires attention, is undergoing change, or in which you would like to see change occur...

3 In your mind's eye, create an iridescent bubble, like a soap bubble, out in front of you...Create a second bubble and place it to the left...Create a third bubble and place it to the right...

4 Assign the bubble on the left to represent yourself...Assign the bubble on the right to represent the other person...The bubble in the center is to represent your relationship communication...

5 Draw a line of light from the bottom of the center relationship bubble down into the earth. This grounding cord begins to clear and release the energy of all past communications up until this point...Misunderstanding and miscommunication wash away...Observe any thoughts, feelings, or sensations that arise...

6 If there is an issue or misunderstanding that needs repair, visualize the conflict as a color and drain it down the grounding cord into the earth...Ask yourself how the communication could have been clearer...Receive the information and then move on...

7 Ask yourself if your heart is ready for change in the relationship...Are you free from any need to control the relationship?...Are you ready to share power?...Does the other person appear ready to share power? If not, what is your next step in this relationship?...

8 As the relationship bubble is cleared and updated, the energy you have invested into the relationship returns to your bubble...The other person's energy returns to his bubble...This redistribution of energy will allow for fresh, clear communication and give room for new emotional and mental investment.

9 Next, choose a color and place it in your bubble...Choose a color to represent the other person and place it in his bubble...Now choose a color to represent the communication between you and the other person, and place it in the relationship bubble...

10 These colors will bring healing...Place in the relationship bubble all the qualities for communication that you would like to have...

Reset the tone of the relationship so that your interactions are for the highest good of each individual.

11 Release the bubble imagery and return your attention to your breath...When you are ready, open your eyes and take a moment to readjust.

Releasing Old Ties

Origin: Native American shamanic tradition.

🚶 **Objective: To release a past relationship**

🕐 **Frequency of use: May be used daily until desired results are achieved**

🕐 **Duration: Sustain practice for 10–15 minutes**

↔ **Cross-references: Use Observing the Breath (page 28)**

① **Difficulty level 1: Technique is easily achieved through practice**

✅ **Complementary treatment: Vital Centers of the Body (page 17)**

According to shaman traditions, cords of energy are formed in the course of building intimate relationships. Through these cords, individuals silently and energetically communicate. These cords can be likened to silk threads that are fine, yet durably strong. The following technique teaches the cutting or breaking of the cords to assist in separation and moving forward.

1 Choose your preferred meditation position... Close your eyes...Engage in Observing the Breath...

2 The "top" of the breath comes at the end of one inhalation and before the next exhalation... The "bottom" of the breath comes at the end of the exhalation and before the next inhalation...Notice the natural pause that occurs at the top and the bottom of the breath...Begin to extend the length of the pauses so that the breath feels circular and never-ending...Relax into the spacious feeling of timelessness...

3 Bring to mind a relationship that you would like to release...Imagine seeing this individual... Notice if he seems close or far away...

4 Imagine that you can see and feel the energy connections through which you have communicated in the past...You may feel the energy connections as yearning, tingling, aching, or burning sensations...You might see the cords as the fine lines of a spider's web connecting the two of you...

5 If you choose to release these cords, take an imaginary knife and gently cut each cord that exists between you and the other person... (If cutting seems too severe, gently twist each cord until it breaks and release it to the other person.)...Take a deep-cleansing breath for each cord that is released...

6 As the cords are released, your life force naturally returns to you as his life force naturally returns to him...

7 Be aware of any sensations that arise as your energy shifts...Affirm that you are ready to release all ties—physical, emotional, mental, and spiritual...As you energetically let go of this other person, ask for a blessing of the highest and greatest good for each of you.

8 Create a bright, golden sun above your head…
Draw the healing light of the sun into your body, directing its energy to the places within which cords were released…The light cleanses and heals these energy centers…

9 Return your attention to the simple inhalation and exhalation of your breath…Notice the top and bottom of each breath…Extend the pauses at the top and bottom of the breath…Feel the weight of your body from head to toe…When you are ready, open your eyes and take a few moments to readjust.

You may modify this meditation to "cleanse" energy cords as opposed to completely breaking them. Follow the above steps. When you come to step 5, create a golden ball of energy. Send this ball through the cords that connect you with the other person. Send the energy ball back and forth through the cords, cleansing them and making communication clearer for you both. Finish with steps 7, 8, and 9.

Trust

The following meditations help enhance trust:

a) Soulstar—Connecting with the "High Self"   b) Enhancing Trust

c) Creating Healthy Boundaries

Soulstar—Connecting with the "High Self"

Origin: Arising from esoteric Christianity practice as an archetype representing the soul, used to remind the practitioner of inner power and the nature of the true self.

Ⓚ **Objective: To deepen trust in a higher power to guide you**

Ⓢ **Frequency of use: Use once a week initially, then daily if desired**

Ⓞ **Duration: Sustain practice for 10–15 minutes**

Ⓗ **Cross-reference: Use Open Palms (page 24) and Abdominal Breathing (page 29)**

① **Difficulty level 2: Requires ability to sustain concentration**

Ⓔ **Complementary treatment: Opening the Heart (page 98)**

There are many levels of consciousness that comprise the self. The Huna tradition, which stems from the ancient esoteric wisdom of Polynesia, views these levels as the "three selves of Huna." The three levels are the basic self, the conscious self, and the high self. The basic self "remembers," the conscious self "imagines," and the high self "inspires."

1 Choose your preferred sitting position. Close your eyes...Engage in Abdominal Breathing...

2 Visualize a bright, white light, 10–12 inches (25–30 cm) directly above your head. This is the soulstar, the light of your high self...The light shines like a thousand points of a brilliant diamond...As you focus on the light, it begins to intensify...

3 Center yourself in the steadiness of this pure and loving light...Draw this light down into your heart center, located at the sternum...The light of your soulstar fills your chest, opening the exquisite flower of your heart.

4 The petals of your heart flower create a cup to catch the dewdrops of the soulstar. The starlight fills your cup with a higher love. The light radiates to envelop you with its benevolence... This light burns steadily, offering security and assurance...This higher light is always available to you to provide guidance and support... Sense that this light is trustworthy and reliable beyond anything or anyone you have experienced previously...

5 The purity and love from this light wash away past hurts and disappointments, offering renewal and hope...Take a few deep breaths to receive this cleansing and to release past experiences...Receive the dewdrops of the soulstar...Trust is not built immediately but unfolds naturally...With time, you come to know and rely upon the integrity of this light to guide you...

6 Release your connection with the light of the soulstar...As the light gently moves away, refocus your attention on the breath...Follow the simple inhalation and exhalation as it helps to integrate the experience of the light...Become aware of your entire body and your external surroundings...Gently open your eyes and take a moment or two to readjust.

Enhancing Trust

Origin: Western; guided imagery approach to assist practitioner in accessing the wisdom and direction of an inner guide.

Objective: To enhance trust in yourself

Frequency of use: May be used regularly

Duration: Sustain practice for 10–15 minutes

Cross-reference: Use Open Palms (page 24) and Focusing on an Object (page 38)

Difficulty level 2: Requires ability to sustain focus

Complementary treatment: Transforming Fear (page 102)

1 Begin in your preferred meditation position. Close your eyes...Place your tongue on the roof of your mouth and engage in Breath Counting.

2 Follow the breath as it leads you to a lighted doorway within your heart...The breath carries you through the doorway and gently places you in a lush field of green...Here you feel a sense of wholeness and connection to all that surrounds you and is within you. Spot a comfortable place to rest and enjoy a few moments of tranquility alone...

3 Look up to see a beautiful presence moving toward you...This is your Inner Guide...The Guide may appear as a male or female, an animal or symbol, or a form of light...

4 As your Guide moves closer, extend an invitation to sit with you...Greet the Guide with reverence and respect...Notice the qualities of wisdom, kindness, and compassion the Guide exudes...What special gifts and abilities does the Inner Guide possess?

5 Tell this wise one that you are seeking information about your ability to trust yourself and others. Ask your Guide a series of questions... Ask the Guide to show you the ways in which you have betrayed your own trust in the past...What steps can you take to foster trust in yourself? Pause to receive any feedback or instruction.

6 Continue your dialogue with your Guide... How can I be more compassionate toward myself?...How can I be more effective in listening to and responding to my needs?...What are the most effective ways to communicate my needs to others? Pause to receive any feedback or instruction.

7 If any other questions arise, ask them now... Thank your Inner Guide for his presence and communication...Bow in respect and reverence...

8 Feel a soft breeze stirring around you...It lifts you up and carries you across the wind back through the doorway of light in your heart...

9 Rest in the wholeness of your heart, pausing for a moment to integrate the information you have received...Return your attention to the breath...When you are ready, open your eyes...You may wish to write down what you recall from your experience.

Creating Healthy Boundaries

Origin: Blend of imagery and Eastern energy practices.

Objective: To help create healthy boundaries to foster trust

Frequency of use: May be used regularly

Duration: Sustain practice for 5–10 minutes

Cross-reference: Use Open Palms (page 24) and Grounding Cord (page 41)

Difficulty level 1: Requires basic ability to visualize

Complementary treatment: Separation Rose (page 111)

Quick remedy

1 Choose your preferred meditation position... Close your eyes...Place your tongue on the roof of your mouth...Follow the natural rhythm of your breath as it drops down deep into your abdomen...

2 Take a moment to establish a connection with your grounding cord...

3 Receive the fullness of the breath deep within your body...Allow the breath to bring cleansing and rejuvenation...With each breath, imagine that you are expanding your ability to accept yourself for who you are in this moment...

4 Create a bright, golden sun, 10–12 inches (25–30 cm) above your head...Reach your hands up to embrace the sun...With your next inhalation, draw the sun into your heart center, located at your sternum...

5 The sun's light radiates from your heart, expanding above your head and beyond your body...Place your hands in front of you, forming a large embrace...Draw imaginary lines of a bubble around this light...Sweep your arms up above your head, then open your arms downward to trace the edges of this bubble...Rest your hands in your lap...This bubble reaches above your head, below your feet, in front and behind you, and to either side to form a protective boundary...

4

6 Bring to mind a time when you felt trusting and peaceful...Imagine someone you hold dear and trust implicitly...If this is challenging, you might use an animal or a role model of someone who represents trustworthiness...Feel his presence at the edge of your bubble, standing guard...

7 In his presence you are completely safe and accepted for who you are...Past hurts and betrayals wash away, leaving you free to experience the possibilities of the present moment...Breathe into the spaciousness of this moment...

8 Recall a painful experience in which you felt your trust was violated...Allow any emotions to resurface...Breathe into this experience, releasing any discomfort down your grounding cord...

9 Consider the crux of the matter...What was the most painful part of your trust being violated?...What negative belief did you form in relation to the experience?...Perhaps it was "I can't trust anyone"...What belief did you form against yourself?...Perhaps it was "I can't trust myself"...or..."I can't trust my judgment."

10 Release the energy of any fear or self-doubt down your grounding cord...Consider what you would have done differently if you had the chance...Would you have said something differently?...Would you have said "No" at the onset?...Release any fear about speaking up for your needs...Imagine having the confidence to say "No," free from fear of rejection or disapproval...

11 Imagine taking baby steps to gradually trust your discretion...See yourself attracting others who are honorable and trustworthy...Be confident in receiving this into your life...

12 When you are ready, return your attention to the simple inhalation and exhalation of your breath...Open your eyes...If you wish, maintain this bubble around you for the rest of your day...

Sex Drive

The action of these poses activates the second energy center, which holds the sexual energy. The following meditations enhance sex drive:

a) Marjarasana—Cat/Cow Pose

b) Recharging and Refining the Sexual Energy

Marjarasana—Cat/Cow Pose

Origin: Pose utilized in a variety of yoga traditions.

🕴 **Objective: To activate and enhance sexual energy**

⟳ **Frequency of use: May be used daily**

🕐 **Duration: Sustain practice for 2–3 minutes**

↔ **Cross-reference: Use Abdominal Breathing (page 29)**

① **Difficulty level 1: Pose is easy to achieve**

🍃 **Complementary treatment: Chakra Cleansing and Balancing (page 34)**

⊕ **Quick remedy**

Marjarasana is an excellent yoga pose to help activate and enhance sexual energy. It opens the energy of the front and back of the second chakra, located between the navel and pubic bone for females and at the pubic bone for males.

Do this exercise barefoot in comfortable clothes on a yoga mat or blanket.

1 Position yourself on your hands and knees. Place your hands directly under your shoulders...Place your knees directly under your hips...Imagine a line running from the back of your neck down your spine to your tailbone...

2 Point your middle fingers straight ahead and press your palms and fingers firmly into the floor. Spread your fingers wide apart if you find this more comfortable...

3 Take a deep breath in, elongating your spine from your head to your tailbone...Look down between your hands...On your next exhalation, tuck your tailbone and arch your back up like a cat... Drop your head and press the middle of your spine up toward the ceiling into the Cat Pose...Hold for three seconds, moving your hips and shoulders as close together as possible...

1

3

4 On your next inhalation, create the opposite movement by looking forward and arching your back down toward the floor...Drop your chest, arch your back slightly, and lift your sitting bones into the Cow Pose...Continue the stretch through your neck by looking upward (as long as this does not strain your neck)...Take three long breaths...

5 Repeat these steps, moving easily between the Cat and Cow Pose...Synchronize your breath to your movements, breathing evenly and naturally through your nose...Repeat the movements in sets of 10 for 2–3 minutes...

4

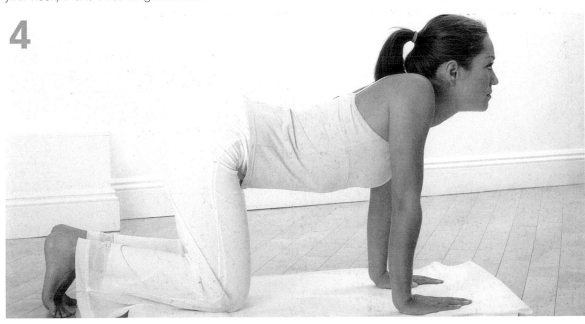

Recharging and Refining the Sexual Energy

Origin: Modified from Taoist tradition, ancient Chinese mystical practices, specifically the microcosmic orbit meditation.

- Objective: To recharge and refine sexual energy
- Frequency of use: May be used daily
- Duration: Sustain pose for 3–5 minutes
- Cross-reference: Use Open Palms (page 24) and Abdominal Breathing (page 29)

- Difficulty level 1: Requires some degree of flexibility
- Complementary treatment: Opening the Heart (page 98)
- Quick remedy

1 Do this exercise barefoot in comfortable clothes...Stand with your feet about hip-width apart...Concentrate on the earth energy...What does the earth energy feel like today? Pick an earth color that pleases you. Visualize this color like a gentle underground spring flowing up through the many layers of the earth...

2 Squat on the floor and place your palms flat on the ground in front of you...Imagine drawing the earth energy into your palms and soles ...Your eyes look softly upward (or forward if this strains your neck) as you simultaneously breathe in the heaven chi...

3 The flow of earth chi moves past the ankles, up the calves, through the knees and thighs, up into the groin area...Here the chi turns into a ball of light...The light permeates your sexual organs... Breathe deeply, visualizing the chi flowing through your sexual organs bringing vitality and rejuvenation...Send the rest of the energy back down into the earth...

4 The continual flow of energy can block your ability to express your sexual energy fully... The earth chi gently cleanses and carries away any energy that has inhibited your sexual experience...

5 Slowly begin to stand upright, moving your hips to the ceiling...Keep a deep bend in your knees so you do not strain the lower back muscles...Try to keep your palms on the floor and your neck soft and relaxed.

6 Inhale and exhale deeply...This forward tipping opens the second chakra, between the solar plexus and pubic bone...allowing the sexual energy to spill out.

This meditation contains the Panj Shabad, one of the most frequently used mantras in the Kundalini (fire) yoga tradition. Its purpose is to tune into the cycle of creation by speaking four primal words of the universe. Sa, Ta, Na, and Ma. The sound Sa represents birth, Ta represents life, Na represents death, and Ma represents rebirth. These sounds are accompanied by specific hand gestures called mudras, which help by sealing your energy into a concentrated state.

7 Inhale and gently return to a squatting position...Repeat this sequence for 3–5 minutes...

8 Release the pose by sitting comfortably on the floor in a simple cross-legged position... Take a few deep breaths to complete the energy circuit.

Creativity

The following meditations promote creativity:

a) Tapping the Universal Creativity   b) Mock-up   c) Clearing the Creative Channels

Tapping the Universal Creativity

Origin: Also referred to as the Panj Shabad, one of the most frequently used mantras in the Kundalini (fire) yoga tradition. Shabad means "word," used in referring to the verbal description of God.

🚶 **Objective: To enhance creative expression**

⟳ **Frequency of use: May be used regularly**

⊙ **Duration: Sustain practice for 5–10 minutes**

↔ **Cross-reference: Use Abdominal Breathing (page 29)**

① **Difficulty level 1: Technique is easily learned**

⊘ **Complementary treatments: Mock-up (page 132) and The Power of Om (page 136)**

⊕ **Quick remedy**

1 Begin in your preferred sitting position. Close your eyes...Focus on your breath to calm your mind and relax your body...Receive the energy of the vital life force throughout your body.

2 If you notice any tension or blocks, simply direct your attention to these places and breathe into them...Feel the breath of life coursing through you... As you clear your body, see yourself as a channel ready to receive the divine life force of creativity...

3 Begin the mudra sequence by bringing the tips of your thumbs and first fingers together (see photo)...This is the first mudra...Breathe into this hand mudra...Bring the tips of your thumbs and middle fingers together to form the second mudra... Pause to breathe...Bring the tips of your thumbs and ring fingers together to form the third mudra...Pause and breathe...Finally, bring the tips of your thumbs and little fingers together to form the fourth mudra.

4 Repeat several times until you feel confident in applying this sequence...Next add the sounds... With the first mudra, say "SA"...With the second mudra, sound "TA"...For the third mudra, say "NA"...And for the fourth mudra, say "MA."

5 Practice doing the mudras with the sounds SA, TA, NA, MA again...SA, TA, NA, MA...Pause with each sound and hand mudra...

3

6 Associate the meanings with the sounds and mudras. SA means birth. TA represents life. NA is for death and MA is for rebirth...Do the mudras with the sounds, thinking "Birth, life, death, rebirth." These words symbolize the universal energies. They represent the cycles of nature and the cycles of creation.

7 Chant this sequence of "SA, TA, NA, MA" out loud in your normal voice for several minutes, pausing between the mudras...

8 Chant "SA, TA, NA, MA" in a whisper for several minutes...

9 Chant "SA, TA, NA, MA" silently for several minutes...

10 Close your meditation with a symbol of gratitude.

10

Mock-up

Origin: Western mysticism meditation to assist in the manifestation of a particular creation.

Objective: To enhance a particular creation

Frequency of use: May be used weekly

Duration: Sustain practice for 10–15 minutes

Cross-reference: Use Open Palms (page 24) and Grounding (page 30)

Difficulty level 2: Requires ability to sustain concentration

Complementary treatment: Prosperity Meditation (page 134)

1 Begin in your preferred meditation position... Close your eyes...Place your tongue on the roof of your mouth...Breathe deeply, directing your breath down into your abdomen...As you exhale, create a grounding connection from your feet to the earth.

2 Visualize the vast expanse of a blue sky on a cloudless day...Touch that blue for just a moment, then let it go...This vastness reminds us that the mind is able to expand to openness...

3 Take a moment to consider what you are choosing to create...Visualize a clear bubble out in front of you...This bubble will be the container for your mock-up.

4 Construct a mental picture of your creation in this bubble...You are the artist...There are no limits to the use of your imagination...Create this picture with as much detail as possible...If you are unclear about the details, simply focus on your general intention for this mock-up...

5 See yourself receiving this creation...Imagine what it will feel like to have this in your life...

6 Give this mock-up bubble a grounding cord by drawing an energetic line from the bottom of the bubble to the earth...Ask that any impediments or blocks to receiving this creation be released from within you and this bubble...Release any internal or external obstacles to receiving this creation...

7 Give this creation a time line of when you hope to receive it...Fill the bubble with brilliant gold universal chi...The gold energy brings this creation to its highest vibratory expression...

8 When you are ready, let go of the bubble as if you were releasing a helium balloon. Watch as the bubble floats out into the center of the universe... Here the energies begin to gather to bring this creation into manifestation.

9 Let go of any intellectual energy that questions how this creation will come about...Release any attachment to this creation; let yourself feel confident that the universe will fully provide...Open your eyes and take a moment to readjust.

Clearing the Creative Channels

Origin: Combination of Hindu and Chinese energy practices to aid in clearing the creative channels of the arms and throat center.

⚉ **Objective: To clear the body's creative channels**

⚉ **Frequency of use: May be used daily**

⚉ **Duration: Sustain practice for 10–15 minutes**

⚉ **Cross-reference: Use Open Palms (page 24) and Observing the Breath (page 28)**

① **Difficulty level 2: Requires ability to sustain focus**

⚉ **Complementary treatment: Chakra Cleansing and Balancing (page 34)**

1 Begin in your preferred meditation posture...Close your eyes...Breathe deeply and draw the light of the universal chi in through the top of your head...The vital energy rejuvenates your body, melting any tension or tightness...

2 The breath becomes a gentle breeze that lifts and carries you to a place in the mind that is calm and untouched by everyday activities and thoughts.

3 Direct your attention to your heart center, located at the sternum...Imagine that you can breathe in and out through this center...The breath ignites a light that glows within your heart...Draw the universal chi into this heart light...The essence of the universe joins your own creative essence...

4 This creative light pumps up from the heart center to the soft indentation between the collarbones...Here is the throat chakra, the center of creative expression...Breathe a bright-blue color into this center, opening the flower of creativity.

5 The creative essence of the flower is released...The blue light flows through the creative channels located behind and across the collarbones...The light clears stagnant or blocked energy...

6 The river of light flows down into the creative channels of the arms...The light flows abundantly, offering a gentle cleansing...As it reaches your hands, the creative energy flows out through your palms and into the bubble around you...

7 The light radiates out to fill your bubble...Enjoy this refreshing energy, soaking up the creative essence through every pore of your aura and body...

8 When you are ready, release your connection with the universal energy...Return your attention to the simple inhalation and exhalation of your breath...Open your eyes and take a moment to readjust.

Prosperity/Abundance

The following meditations help increase the energies of prosperity and abundance:

a) Prosperity Meditation   b) Gratitude Meditation   c) The Power of Om

Prosperity Meditation

Origin: Ancient Eastern Indian mudra. Mudras are sacred hand positions. The Gyana Mudra (pronounced yawn-ah moo-dra) or the Mudra of Knowledge is used in this meditation to invoke and seal the energy of prosperity.

Ⓚ **Objective: To enhance the flow of prosperity and abundance**

Ⓢ **Frequency of use: May be used regularly**

Ⓞ **Duration: Sustain practice for 10–12 minutes, repeating as necessary**

↔ **Cross-reference: Use Abdominal Breathing (page 29) and Mudra of Knowledge (page 25)**

① **Difficulty level 1: Technique is easy to apply**

✺ **Complementary treatment: Mock-up (page 132)**

✚ **Quick remedy when used regularly**

The Mudra of Knowledge (Gyana Mudra) is used in this meditation to invoke and seal the energy of prosperity.

1 Choose your preferred meditation position...Rest with your eyes closed and your tongue on the roof of your mouth...Engage in Abdominal Breathing...

2 When you feel sufficiently relaxed, place your forefingers and thumbs in the Mudra of Knowledge position. Tuck your thumbs under the forefingers to make the mudra receptive... This signifies the joining of individual and cosmic consciousness. The receptive symbol represents "inviting the teacher," used in this way to invite the creative essence that lies within.

3 With both hands in the mudra position, cross the right hand in front of the left hand...Place both hands in front of the heart center, located in the chest...Breathe deeply, receiving the creative life force into your hands...

4 Hold what you are choosing to create firmly in your mind...Imagine a lush field of green... Use the green to symbolize prosperity...A wind washes over the field carrying prosperity to your heart...Breathe into the image that you are striving to receive...Make this creation as real as possible. Engage all your senses. Give yourself permission to bring it into form...See yourself receiving it... The emotion of your heart moves you toward this manifestation...

5 Open your fingers and place your palms upright with your left hand over your right...Hold your hands over your heart center...Repeat the sacred sound of Om three times, out loud or silently. Open your eyes and take a moment to readjust.

Gratitude Meditation

Origin: Gesture of gratitude found in both Western and Eastern practice.

(⚹) **Objective: To cultivate prosperity through gratitude**

(⟳) **Frequency of use: May be used daily**

(⊙) **Duration: Sustain practice for 5 minutes or longer**

(↔) **Cross-reference: Use Open Palms (page 24) and Abdominal Breathing (page 29)**

(1) **Difficulty level 1: Technique is easy to execute**

(⊘) **Complementary treatment: Tapping the Universal Creativity (page 130)**

(+) **Quick remedy**

1 Begin in your preferred meditation position. Close your eyes...Place your tongue on the roof of your mouth...Focus on your breath through Abdominal Breathing...

2 When you feel sufficiently relaxed, turn your attention to your heart center, located at your sternum...Visualize a lush green color radiating from your heart...Imagine that you can breathe in and out through your heart center...Luminous green radiates out into your body with each breath...

3 Bring to mind someone in your life you are grateful for...Hold their image in your mind's eye...Create a symbol of appreciation and send this to him from your heart...

4 Reflect upon an aspect of your work you are grateful for...Create a symbol and hold it in your heart...Breathe the quality of gratitude into this symbol, giving thanks for all that you value.

5 Consider a challenging circumstance... Hold an image of this in your heart... Notice any pain or discomfort surrounding this circumstance...Breathe into this image, allowing space for acceptance...Silently give thanks for this opportunity and ask for guidance to meet this challenge...

6 Now take a few minutes to express gratitude for all other aspects of your life you wish to express...No facet of your life is too small to acknowledge appreciation for.

7 When you are ready, return your attention to the simple inhalation and exhalation of your breath...Choose a closing gesture, such as hands in prayer position, to express appreciation for all that you received in the meditation. Open your eyes and take a moment to readjust.

The Power of Om

Origin: Om, pronounced "home" without the h, is the sacred and foremost symbol of the ancient Sanskrit language. When the tone of Om is sounded as a mantra, it brings about our conscious intention. When spoken with clarity and concentration, Om has the ability to materialize that which you are seeking.

(🚶) **Objective: To enhance prosperity and abundance**

(⏱) **Frequency of use: May be used daily**

(🕐) **Duration: Sustain pose for 5 minutes, repeating as desired**

(↔) **Cross-reference: Use Open Palms (page 24)**

(1) **Difficulty level 1: Technique is easy to carry out**

(🌿) **Complementary treatment: Tapping the Universal Creativity (page 130)**

(✛) **Quick remedy**

Om, pronounced "home" without the h, is the sacred and foremost symbol of the ancient Sanskrit language. It has been said that the universe recognizes two words: Om and Yes. Om resonates with the infinite power of creation. When the tone of Om is sounded as a mantra, it brings about our conscious intention. The universe supports what we are striving to create. The sound is spoken as a chant and prolonged indefinitely.

Receiving Abundance

1 Choose your preferred sitting position...Sit with a straight spine...Close your eyes...Place your tongue on the roof of your mouth and breathe deeply...

2 Take a moment to center yourself, focusing on the expansiveness of the breath...

3 Mentally create a symbol that represents prosperity and abundance...Hold that image in your heart...Breathe into the symbol...Engage all of your senses in realizing this abundance...Notice the sensations that arise...Perhaps it is the sensation of excitement...Peace...Glad expectancy...Pleasurable anticipation...Breathe into these feelings...

4 Visualize your heart center, located at the center of your chest, as a beautiful green brightness... Imagine that you can breathe in and out of your heart center...Feel abundance spreading throughout your body with each breath...

5 Bring your hands up level with your heart center. Cup your hands with palms facing upward and little fingers side by side...Your hands fill with the creative energies of the universe... Receive this abundance with gratitude, breathing it into your body...

6 Close the meditation with the affirmation of Om. Sound the Om three times, silently or out loud, letting the sound extend indefinitely each time...

Five-Pointed Star

1 Begin this pose by standing barefoot with your feet wide apart...Lift your arms up to mimic your feet so that you are creating the shape of a star...

2 Place your tongue on the roof of your mouth... Take in three cleansing breaths through your nose...

3 Reach your arms up high in a gesture of receiving...Press your feet firmly into the floor to represent grounding and physical manifestation...

4 Direct your attention to your heart center, located at the sternum...Imagine breathing in and out of your heart center...The breath of life enters and exits from this center...

5 Hold in your heart a symbol of abundance and prosperity...Breathe the universal chi into this symbol...Feel the chi coming in through your head and arms and moving into your heart...

6 Take the energy of abundance into your heart and direct it down to your legs (this symbolizes manifesting it in the physical plane)...Channel this energy from the cosmos, to the heart, through the symbol, and down through your legs for 10 cycles of breath...

7 Close by sounding the Om three times, silently or out loud. As you sound the Om, draw your hands to your heart, then reach them up toward the sky again for the next Om.

Bibliography/ Recommended Reading

Bailey, Alice A. *Esoteric Healing*. New York: Lucis Publishing Co., 1953.

Benson, Herbert, M.D. *The Relaxation Response*. New York: Harper Torch, 2000

Bourne, Edmund J.,Ph.D. *The Anxiety and Phobia Workbook*. Oakland, California: New Harbinger, 1990.

Bradshaw, John. *Homecoming; Reclaiming and Championing Your Inner Child*. Florida: Health Communications, Inc., 1992

Brennan, Barbara Ann. *Hands of Light*. New York: Bantam Books, 1987.

Carrington, Patricia. *Freedom in Meditation*. New York: Anchor Press/Doubleday, 1978.

Chia, Mantak. *Awaken Healing Energy through the Tao*. New Mexico: Aurora Press, 1983.

Chikly, Bruno, M.D. *Lymph Drainage Therapy I; Study Guide*. International Alliance for Health Educators, 1996.

Chodron, Pema. *The Places that Scare You*. Boston and London: Shambhala Publications, 2001.

Chuen, Master Lam Kam. *Chi Kung; The Way of Healing*. New York: Broadway Books, 1999.

Cleary, Thomas. *Zen Essence; The Science of Freedom*. Boston and London: Shambhala Publications, 1989.

Csikszentmihalyi, Mihaly. *Flow: The Psychology of Optimal Experience*. New York: Harper & Row, 1990

Dalai Lama. *How to Practice; The Way to a Meaningful Life*. New York: Pocket Book, 2002

Farhi, Donna. *The Breathing Book*. New York: Henry Holt & Company, 1996

Fleischmann, Robert, and Japikse, Carol. *Active Meditation*. Cincinnati, Ohio: Ariel Press, 1982.

Haich, Elisabeth. *Initiation*. New Mexico: Aurora Press, Inc., 2000

Hay, Louise L. *You Can Heal Your Life*. Carlsbad, California: Hay House, Inc. 1984

Jahnke, Roger O.M.D. *The Healing Promise of Qi*. Chicago: Contemporary Books, 2002.

Kabat-Zinn, Jon. *Wherever You Go, There you Are*. New York: Hyperion, 1995.

Knaster, Mirka. *Discovering the Body's Wisdom*. New York: Bantam Books, 1996.

McDonald, Kathleen. *How to Meditate; A Practical Guide*. London: Wisdom Publications, 1984.

McKay, Matthew, Ph.D, Fanning, Patrick and Paleg,Kim, Ph.D. *Couple Skills*. Oakland, California: New Harbinger, 1994.

Myss, Caroline, Ph.D. *Anatomy of the Spirit*. New York and Ontario: Three Rivers Press, 1996

Northrup, Christiane, M.D. *Women's Bodies. Women's Wisdom*, New York; Bantam Books, 1998.

Parrish-Hara, Carol. *Adventure in Meditation, Volumes I & II*. Tahequah, Oklahoma: Sparrow Hawk Press, 1995, 1996.

Parrish-Hara, Carol. *The New Dictionary of Spiritual Thought*. Tahlequah, Oklahoma: Sparrow Hawk Press, 2002

Pearsall, Paul. *The Heart's Code*. New York: Broadway Books, 1998

Powell, A. E. *The Astral Body*. Wheaton, Illinois: The Theosophical Publishing House, 1927.

Santorelli, Saki. *Heal Thy Self; Lessons on Mindfulness in Medicine*. New York: Bell Tower, 2000.

Siegel, Bernie, M.D. *Love, Medicine and Miracles*. New York: Perennial, 1998.

Singh, Dharam. *The Kundalini Experience; Bringing Body, Mind and Spirit Together*. Fireside Publishing, 2002

Tulku, Tarthang. *Tibetan Relaxation*. London: Duncan Baird Publishers, 2003.

Vaughan-Lee, Llewellyn. *Sufism; The Transformation of the Heart*. Inverness, California: The Golden Sufi Center, 1995

Zukav, Gary, and Francis, Linda. *The Heart of the Soul*. New York: Simon & Schuster, 2001.

Acknowledgments

The author wishes to The author wishes to extend her grateful acknowledgment to Martin Barnes, Carol Parrish-Hara, Janet Weiss Quate, and her publishers Collins & Brown; also to her yoga teachers Laura Mahr and Kristine Kaoverii Weber, and to all her meditation students.

I bow to the divine in you, Namaste.

The publishers wish to thank:

Dr Lenington for writing the Foreword

Kang Chen for creating the symbols

Trina D. for the illustrations

Yoga Matters for supplying the model's clothing
32 Clarendon Road
London
N8 0DJ
+44 (0) 20 8888 8588
www.yogamatters.com

About the author

Martina Glasscock Barnes, M.S., is a licensed professional counselor and has been a student and teacher of meditation since 1982. She is the author of *Meditation for the Western Mind* and numerous audio products on health and wellness-based meditation. Formerly the head meditation teacher at the Berkeley Psychic Institute in Berkeley, California, Martina went on to study at the internationally acclaimed Sancta Sophia mystery school. Her teachings draw on the rich traditions of Eastern and Western mysticism to convey an approach that is both practical and profound. She works as a psychotherapist in private practice and as a volunteer grief counselor at a nonprofit hospice in Asheville, North Carolina.

About Dr. Lenington

Ken Lenington, M.D., is certified by the American Board of Psychiatry. He received his degree from the Medical College of Wisconsin in 1977. Dr. Lenington has practiced general psychiatry for over 20 years, serving as medical director for both psychiatric facilities and hospitals. He has been awarded the Exemplary Psychiatrist Award by the National Alliance for the Mentally Ill (NAMI). The use of biological and psycho-spiritual therapies in a complementary manner is an ongoing interest and a fundamental part of his current practice. Dr. Lenington began using meditation techniques himself in 1983 and continues to do so today.

Index